Crystallization-Study
of
1 Corinthians

Volume One

Witness Lee

The Holy Word for Morning Revival

Living Stream Ministry
Anaheim, California

First Edition, January 2003.

ISBN 0-7363-2073-3
ISBN 0-7363-2072-5 (two-volume set)

Published by

Living Stream Ministry
2431 W. La Palma Ave., Anaheim, CA 92801 U.S.A.
P. O. Box 2121, Anaheim, CA 92814 U.S.A.

Printed in the United States of America

03 04 05 06 07 08 09 / 10 9 8 7 6 5 4 3 2 1

Contents

Preface

1. This book is intended as an aid to believers in developing a daily time of morning revival with the Lord in His word. At the same time, it provides a review of the 2002 Winter Training on the "Crystallization-study of 1 Corinthians." Through intimate contact with the Lord in His word, the believers can be constituted with life and truth and thereby equipped to prophesy in the meetings of the church unto the building up of the Body of Christ.

2. The content of this book is taken primarily from the *Crystallization-study Outlines,* the text and footnotes of the Recovery Version of the Bible, selections from the writings of Watchman Nee and Witness Lee, and *Hymns,* all of which are published by Living Stream Ministry.

3. The book is divided into weeks. One training message is covered per week. Each week first presents the message outline, followed by six daily portions, a hymn, and then some space for writing. The message outline has been divided into days, corresponding to the six daily portions. Each daily portion covers certain points and begins with a section entitled "Morning Nourishment." This section contains selected verses and a short reading that can provide rich spiritual nourishment through intimate fellowship with the Lord. The "Morning Nourishment" is followed by a section entitled "Today's Reading," a longer portion of ministry related to the day's main points. Each day's portion concludes with a short list of references for further reading and some space for the saints to make notes concerning their spiritual inspiration, enlightenment, and enjoyment to serve as a reminder of what they have received of the Lord that day.

4. The space provided at the end of each week is for composing a short prophecy. This prophecy can be composed by considering all our daily notes, the "harvest" of our inspirations during the week, and preparing a main point with some sub-points to be spoken in the church meetings for the organic building up of the Body of Christ.

5. The *Crystallization-study Outlines* were compiled by Living Stream Ministry from the writings of Watchman Nee and Witness Lee. The outlines, footnotes, and references in the Recovery Version of the Bible were written by Witness Lee. All of the other references cited in this publication are from the ministry of Watchman Nee and Witness Lee.

2002 Winter Training

CRYSTALLIZATION-STUDY
OF 1 CORINTHIANS

Banners:

God has called us into the fellowship of His Son
that we may partake of Christ and enjoy Him
as our unique center and as our God-given portion.

The enjoyment of the crucified Christ
as the life-giving Spirit in our spirit
solves all the problems in the church
and issues in the growth in life
for the building up of the church.

The essence of the New Testament is the two spirits—
the divine Spirit and the human spirit—
mingled together as one spirit.

Love is the most excellent way
and prophesying is the excelling gift
for the building up of the church.

Called into the Fellowship of God's Son— the Enjoyment of the All-inclusive Christ

Scripture Reading: 1 Cor. 1:1-13

Day 1

I. The essential and underlying thought of 1 Corinthians is that we should enjoy Christ (10:3-4).

II. The underlying thought of 1 Corinthians 1 and 2 is that we must drop everything except Christ and take Christ as everything to us (2:2).

III. "To the church of God which is in Corinth, to those who have been sanctified in Christ Jesus, the called saints, with all those who call upon the name of our Lord Jesus Christ in every place, who is theirs and ours" (1:2):

A. Christ, the all-inclusive One, belongs to all believers; He is our portion given to us by God (Col. 1:12).

B. In 1 Corinthians 1:2 *theirs and ours* emphasizes the fact of Christ being the unique center of all believers in whatever place or situation.

C. First Corinthians reveals that God has given to us the all-inclusive Christ, with the riches of at least twenty items, as our unique portion for our enjoyment (vv. 24, 30; 2:8, 10; 3:11; 5:7-8; 10:3-4; 11:3; 12:12; 15:20, 23, 47, 45).

D. God has determined that in His economy one person—His Son, the Lord Jesus Christ— must be everything to all the believers (Matt. 17:5; Col. 3:11).

E. In His economy God's intention is to give Christ to us as our portion and to work Christ into us (Gal. 1:15-16; 2:20; 4:19; Eph. 3:17a).

F. We should focus on Christ as our unique center appointed by God that all the problems among the believers may be solved.

Day 2   IV. **"God is faithful, through whom you were called into the fellowship of His Son, Jesus Christ our Lord" (1 Cor. 1:9):**

A. God has called us into the fellowship of His Son that we may partake of Christ, participate in Him, and enjoy Him as our God-given portion.

B. God has called us into the fellowship of, the participation in, the all-inclusive Christ; all believers should be focused on Him, not being distracted by any gifted person, any over-stressed doctrine, or any particular practice.

C. Fellowship means that we and Christ have become one (6:17):

   1. We have been called into a oneness where we are one with Him and He is one with us.

   2. The word *joined* in 6:17 is a synonym for *fellowship* in 1:9; the joining is actually the fellowship.

   3. Whenever we are one spirit with the Lord, we are in the fellowship of Christ, and we experience Him as the all-inclusive One.

Day 3   D. Fellowship means that we enjoy Christ and all He is and that He enjoys us and all we are (Phil. 1:18; 2:17-18, 28; 3:1; 4:4, 10):

   1. We have been called into a mutuality in which we enjoy what the Son of God is and He enjoys what we are.

   2. This fellowship implies a wonderful, universal, mutual enjoyment—our enjoyment of the Triune God, the Triune God's enjoyment of us, and the enjoyment which the believers have with one another.

Day 4   E. The fellowship of Christ becomes the fellowship the apostles shared with the believers in Christ in His Body, the church (Acts 2:42; 1 John 1:3):

   1. This is the fellowship that we enjoy in partaking of His blood and His body at His table (1 Cor. 10:16, 21).

    2. Such a fellowship must be unique because He is unique; it forbids any division among the members of His unique Body (12:27).

    3. This fellowship involves not only the oneness between us and the Triune God but also the oneness among all the believers (John 17:21-23; Eph. 4:3).

F. The fellowship of Christ is actually carried out by the Spirit; thus, in our experience the fellowship of the Son is the fellowship of the Spirit (2 Cor. 13:14; Phil. 2:1).

G. Fellowship also implies a mutual flowing among the believers (1 John 1:3):

    1. In the New Testament fellowship describes the flowing both between us and the Lord and between us and one another (Phil. 2:1).

    2. The flow, the current, we have in our spiritual fellowship involves both oneness and life; our fellowship is a flow of oneness.

    3. This fellowship is the reality of the church life (1 Cor. 1:9, 2).

Day 5

H. Our only preference must be Christ as the unique center, the Christ who is theirs and ours, the Christ into whose fellowship we have been called by God:

    1. To have a preference is to lose Christ as the unique center and to be in the flesh (vv. 2, 9, 11-13; 3:1-4).

    2. The all-inclusive Christ is our unique choice, preference, portion, taste, and enjoyment (1:24, 30; 2:2).

    3. We must exalt only one name—the name of our Lord Jesus Christ, the name of the wonderful, all-inclusive One into whose fellowship God has called us (Phil. 2:9-11; Eph. 1:21).

    4. Only one thing can keep us from division—the realization that the all-inclusive Christ is our portion and that we have been

called into the fellowship, the enjoyment, of such a One (Col. 1:12; 2:9, 16-17; 3:11).

V. "Now I beseech you, brothers, through the name of our Lord Jesus Christ, that you all speak the same thing and that there be no divisions among you, but that you be attuned in the same mind and in the same opinion" (1 Cor. 1:10):

A. Speaking differently is a predominant characteristic of fallen man; the desire of God is that all His saved and redeemed people speak the same thing.

B. If we would be attuned to the same mind and in the same opinion, we need to have a vision of the place of Christ in God's economy (Col. 3:11).

C. If we see the all-inclusive Christ and learn the secret of enjoying Him, our way of thinking and speaking will be changed (Phil. 2:2, 5; 3:15; Rom. 15:6).

D. The only way to avoid division is to see Christ, receive Christ, and enjoy Christ; this and only this will cause us to be attuned to the same mind and in the same opinion.

Morning Nourishment

1 Cor. For I did not determine to know anything among
2:2 you except Jesus Christ, and this One crucified.

1:2 To the church of God which is in Corinth, to those
who have been sanctified in Christ Jesus, the
called saints, with all those who call upon the
name of our Lord Jesus Christ in every place,
who is theirs and ours.

Col. Giving thanks to the Father, who has qualified
1:12 you for a share of the allotted portion of the
saints in the light.

The underlying concept of 1 Corinthians 1 and 2 is that we
must drop everything except Christ. When Paul came to Corinth
and preached Christ, he determined not to know anything among
them except Jesus Christ and this One crucified. This indicates
clearly that he forsook everything except Christ. As we read
1 Corinthians, we need to be deeply impressed with this underlying thought. We need to see that we must drop everything but
Christ and genuinely take Christ as everything to us. Christ
truly is all-inclusive; He is everything, even the depths of God.

In 1:2 Paul says that the Lord Jesus Christ is "theirs and
ours." Christ as the all-inclusive One belongs to all believers.
He is our portion given to us by God (Col. 1:12). The apostle
added this special phrase at the end of this verse to stress the
crucial fact of Christ's being the unique center of all believers
in whatever place or situation. In this Epistle the apostle's
intention was to solve the problems existing among the saints
in Corinth. For all the problems, especially the matter of division, the only solution is the all-inclusive Christ. We have all
been called into the fellowship, the participation, in Him (1 Cor.
1:9). All believers should be focused on Him, not distracted by
any gifted person, any overemphasis on doctrine, or any particular practice. (*Life-study of 1 Corinthians,* pp. 152, 16)

Today's Reading

First Corinthians unveils to us that the very Christ, who is the portion of all believers, and into whose fellowship we have been called, is all-inclusive. He is God's power and God's wisdom as righteousness, sanctification, and redemption to us (1:24, 30). He is our glory for our glorification (2:7; Rom. 8:30), hence, the Lord of glory (1 Cor. 2:8). He is the depths of God, the deep things of God (2:10). He is the unique foundation of God's building (3:11). He is our Passover (5:7), the unleavened bread (5:8), the spiritual food, the spiritual drink, and the spiritual rock (10:3-4). He is the Head (11:3) and the Body (12:12). He is the firstfruits (15:20, 23), the second Man (15:47), and the last Adam (15:45); as such, He became the life-giving Spirit (15:45). This all-inclusive One, with the riches of at least nineteen items, God has given to us as our portion for our enjoyment. We should concentrate on Him, not on any persons, things, or matters other than Him. We should focus on Him as our unique center appointed by God that all the problems among the believers may be solved. It is into the fellowship of such a One that we have been called by God. This fellowship of Him becomes the fellowship the apostles shared with the believers (Acts 2:42; 1 John 1:3) in His Body, the church, and should be the fellowship we enjoy in the partaking of His blood and His body at His table (1 Cor. 10:16, 21). Such a fellowship must be unique, because He is unique. It forbids any division among the members of His unique Body.

In 1:1-9 Paul impresses us with the fact that in God's economy Christ is the unique center. God's intention is to make Christ His Son the center of His economy and also to make Him everything to all the believers. This is why Paul tells us in verse 9 that we have been called into the fellowship of the Son, Jesus Christ our Lord. It is also the reason he points out in verse 2 that Christ is both theirs and ours. In His economy God's intention is to make Christ everything, to give Christ to us as our portion, and also to work Christ into us. (*Life-study of 1 Corinthians,* pp. 23-24, 29-30)

Further Reading: Life-study of 1 Corinthians, msgs. 2-3, 5, 10-12

Enlightenment and inspiration: _____
_____
_____
_____

Morning Nourishment

1 Cor. God is faithful, through whom you were called into
1:9 the fellowship of His Son, Jesus Christ our Lord.
6:17 But he who is joined to the Lord is one spirit.

[First Corinthians 1:9] tells us that God has called us into
the fellowship of His Son, Jesus Christ our Lord. Fellowship
denotes the partaking of, the participation in, God's Son. It is to
partake of, participate in, the all-inclusive Christ. God has
called us into such a fellowship that we may partake of Christ,
participate in Him, and enjoy Him as our God-given portion.
This word, like the word concerning Christ's being theirs and
ours in verse 2, stresses again the crucial fact of Christ's being
the unique center of the believers for the solving of the problems
among them, especially that of division. (*Life-study of 1 Corinthians,* p. 23)

Today's Reading

In [1 Corinthians] 6:17 Paul says that "he who is joined to
the Lord is one spirit." The word *joined* in this verse is a
synonym for *fellowship* in 1:9. Fellowship and being joined refer
to the same matter....The joining is actually the fellowship. This
enables us to see the connection between 1:2 and 9 and 6:17.
The word *called* in 1:9 connects that verse with 1:2, and the
word *joined* in 6:17 connects that verse with 1:9.

The way to enjoy the Lord experientially is through Him as the
Spirit in our spirit. Today Christ is the life-giving Spirit, and we
have a regenerated human spirit. When we are joined to Him, we
become one spirit with Him. Whenever we are one spirit with the
Lord, we are in the fellowship of Christ. Furthermore, when we
exercise our spirit to call on the name of the Lord Jesus, we apply
this fellowship and enjoy Christ. What a rich enjoyment this is!

The all-inclusive Christ is our portion and that we have been
called into the fellowship of this Christ. But how can the
incarnated, crucified, and resurrected Christ become our portion for our enjoyment? To understand this we need to consider
6:17....The fellowship into which we have been called is Christ

as the life-giving Spirit. To experience this fellowship we must be one spirit with Him. In our spirit we are one with the life-giving Spirit.

Suppose a brother comes to you with complaints about his wife. The brother may say, "The Lord has given you a wife who is kind, gentle, patient, and loving. But my wife is extremely difficult to live with. If your wife were like mine, you would probably be in a worse situation than I am concerning married life. I simply have no way to go on with my wife. What shall I do?" The best way to help such a brother is not to explain matters to him or argue with him…[or] give him more doctrinal concepts. His urgent need is to realize that he is one spirit with the Lord. However, it is difficult to help a brother in such a situation to see that he is one spirit with the Lord and that he should call on the name of the Lord. But if you can help this brother understand that he is one spirit with the life-giving Spirit, and if you can help him call on the Lord, that brother's living will be revolutionized.

As many of us can testify, when we exercise our spirit and call on the name of the Lord, we enjoy His sweetness. At times we may weep because the Lord touches us in a very tender way. At other times praises may burst forth, and we may thank the Lord for giving us the best and most suitable wife or husband. If we call on the name of the Lord by exercising our spirit, we shall immediately realize that God has given us the best mate. May more and more among us have this kind of experience.

Christ is both theirs and ours, and we have been called into the fellowship of this Christ. This fellowship takes place only in the spirit. Praise the Lord that he who is joined to Him is one spirit! Therefore, we have a source, a fountain, and an inexhaustible reservoir. This source is Christ, the processed Triune God, the all-inclusive life-giving Spirit. (*Life-study of 1 Corinthians,* pp. 93, 108-109, 111-112)

Further Reading: Life-study of 1 Corinthians, msgs. 3, 10, 12

Enlightenment and inspiration: _____

_____

_____

_____

Morning Nourishment

1 Cor. God is faithful, through whom you were called into
1:9 the fellowship of His Son, Jesus Christ our Lord.
Phil. And in like manner you also rejoice, and you re-
2:18 joice together with me.
4:4 Rejoice in the Lord always; again I will say, rejoice.

This word *fellowship* is profound and very deep. I do not
believe that any Christian teacher or expositor of the Bible can
exhaust the meaning of this word. Fellowship does not merely
mean that there is communication between you and someone
else; it also denotes participation in that one. Furthermore, it
means that we and Christ have become one. It also means that
we enjoy Christ and all He is, and that He enjoys us and what
we are. As a result, there is not only a mutual communication,
but a mutuality in every way. All that Christ is becomes ours,
and all that we are becomes His....We have been called into the
fellowship of God's Son. We have been called into a mutuality in
which we enjoy what the Son of God is, and in which we are one
with Him and He is one with us....In 1 Corinthians 6:17, Paul says,
"He who is joined to the Lord is one spirit." We have been called
into such a oneness. In this oneness we enjoy what Christ is, and
He enjoys what we are. (*Life-study of 1 Corinthians*, pp. 24-25)

Today's Reading

It is not easy to give an adequate definition of the fellowship
of the Son of God. This matter is altogether wonderful. This
fellowship involves not only the oneness between us and the
Triune God, but also the oneness among all the believers.
Furthermore, it implies enjoyment—our enjoyment of the Triune God, the Triune God's enjoyment of us, and also the enjoyment, which the believers have with one another. In this
fellowship we enjoy the Triune God, and the Triune God enjoys
us. Moreover, we enjoy all the believers, and all the believers
enjoy us. What a wonderful, universal, mutual enjoyment! We
have been called into something which is termed the fellowship
of God's Son. This fellowship is universal and mutual. The

mutuality of this fellowship is not only between the believers and the Triune God, but also among the believers themselves.

Because we have been called into such a fellowship, we should not say that we are of Paul, of Cephas, of Apollos, or of any other person. Neither should we say that we are of a certain doctrine or of a particular practice. God has not called us into the fellowship of persons, doctrines, and practices. We have not been called into the fellowship of Paul or of anyone else; neither have we been called into a fellowship related to a doctrine or practice. We have been called uniquely into the fellowship of God's Son. This means that we have been called into the reality, the embodiment, of the Triune God. In this fellowship we enjoy the Triune God—the Father, the Son, and the Spirit. In this fellowship we also enjoy all the believers, and the believers enjoy us. Furthermore, the Triune God enjoys us and all the other believers in every place.

In 1 Corinthians 1:9 Paul says that God has called us into the fellowship of His Son. The meaning of the word fellowship is deep and profound. The New Testament illustrates this fellowship by a feast. In the Gospels the Lord Jesus said that a feast had been prepared and that people were invited to it (Matt. 22:1-3; Luke 14:16-17). We all have been invited to a marvelous feast. Here at the feast we are enjoying course after course. This enjoyment of the feast is a mutual participation, a co-participation. Thus, in the fellowship of God's Son we have enjoyment. This enjoyment, however, is corporate, not individualistic. As we enjoy this feast together, we have fellowship, communion.

Some versions translate the Greek word for fellowship, *koinonia,* as communion. Fellowship definitely implies communion. To have communion is to share something in common. When you eat breakfast alone, you do not enjoy communion. But when you…enjoy [a] feast with [a large number of people], you have communion. This communion is a co-enjoyment, a co-participation. (*Life-study of 1 Corinthians,* pp. 30-31, 100)

Further Reading: Life-study of 1 Corinthians, msgs. 3-4, 11

Enlightenment and inspiration: _____

_____

_____

_____

Morning Nourishment

Acts And they continued steadfastly in the teaching
2:42 and the fellowship of the apostles, in the breaking
of bread and the prayers.

1 John That which we have seen and heard we report also
1:3 to you that you also may have fellowship with us,
and indeed our fellowship is with the Father and
with His Son Jesus Christ.

2 Cor. The grace of the Lord Jesus Christ and the love of
13:14 God and the fellowship of the Holy Spirit be with
you all.

The word *fellowship* is used for the first time in Acts 2:42,
where we are told that those who were saved and added to the
church on the day of Pentecost continued steadfastly in the
teaching and the fellowship of the apostles. The apostles had
preached the gospel to them, and this gospel preaching brought
them into something which the Bible calls fellowship.

I doubt that there is in any language an equivalent of the
Greek word for fellowship, *koinonia*. This word implies oneness
and also a mutual flowing among the believers. When we enjoy
fellowship with one another, there is a flow among us. Although
electrical current is not living, it can be used to illustrate what
we mean by a flow in fellowship. The flowing of electricity
produces oneness. The flow, the current, we have in our spiritual
fellowship involves both oneness and life. Our fellowship is a
flow in oneness; it is an intercommunication among us as
believers in Christ.

In the New Testament, fellowship describes both the flowing
between us and the Lord and between us and one another
[1 John 1:3]....In 1 John we have life (1:1-2) and then fellowship.
There is a flow, a current, vertically between us and the Father
and the Son and horizontally between us and other believers.
Praise the Lord that on earth today there is something called
fellowship, a fellowship among the children of God and a
fellowship of the children of God with the Triune God! (*Life-
study of 1 Corinthians*, p. 124)

Today's Reading

According to Paul's word in [1 Corinthians] 1:9, we all have been called by God into this fellowship. Perhaps the best illustration of fellowship is the circulation of blood in the human body. Right now the blood is circulating throughout your body.... Life depends on this circulation. Just as there is the circulation of blood in the human body, so there is a spiritual circulation, called the fellowship, in the Body of Christ....It is crucial for us to realize that in the Lord's recovery we are being brought back into this flow, into this fellowship.

From 1:9 we see that through the faithful God we have been called into the fellowship of the Son of God, Jesus Christ. This indicates clearly that we have not been called into the fellowship of any denomination, practice, or theological doctrine. The unique fellowship into which God has called us is the fellowship of His Son. This means that He alone must be our fellowship.

The Corinthians were divided by their preferences and choices. Paul, however, wanted them to realize that they had been called into one fellowship. This means that they had been called into one participation, one appreciation, one enjoyment, one preference, one choice. Those who said, "I am of Paul," appreciated Paul and enjoyed him. The same was true of those who said that they were of Apollos or of Cephas. But the fellowship in 1:9 is our participation in Christ; it is our enjoyment and appreciation of Him and our preference for Him. In these verses Paul seems to be saying to the believers at Corinth, "Don't say that you are of this person or of that person. You all must realize that you have been called into one enjoyment, appreciation, preference, and choice. You have been called into one fellowship, and this is the Son of God as our portion. We all are in the fellowship of Christ." (*Life-study of 1 Corinthians,* pp. 125-126)

Further Reading: Life-study of 1 Corinthians, msgs. 12, 14

Enlightenment and inspiration: _____

_____

_____

_____

Morning Nourishment

1 Cor. To the church of God which is in Corinth, to those
  1:2 who have been sanctified in Christ Jesus, the
       called saints, with all those who call upon the name
       of our Lord Jesus Christ in every place, *who is*
       theirs and ours.
  9-10 God is faithful, through whom you were called into
       the fellowship of His Son, Jesus Christ our Lord.
       Now I beseech you, brothers, through the name of
       our Lord Jesus Christ, that you all speak the same
       thing and *that* there be no divisions among you,
       but *that* you be attuned in the same mind and in
       the same opinion.
   12 Now I mean this, that each of you says, I am of Paul,
       and I of Apollos, and I of Cephas, and I of Christ.

All believers in Christ, including us, have their preferences.
The Corinthian believers had theirs....Preferences are fleshly.
As long as you hold to your preference, you are in the flesh.
Furthermore, having a preference causes you to lose Christ as
the unique center. Our unique center is the Lord who is both
theirs and ours, the Son of God into whose fellowship we all
have been called of God. We have not been called into our
preference, either in elders or in local churches. Sometimes
saints have said, "I am not happy with the church here, and I
don't want to stay here any longer. I intend to move to another
locality." This is to have a preference, and it is fleshly. To repeat,
to have a preference is to lose Christ as the unique center.
(*Life-study of 1 Corinthians,* pp. 25-26)

Today's Reading

I believe that as Paul was writing this Epistle to the Corinthian believers, he was saying, "Dear brothers and sisters, you
need to realize that neither Paul, Cephas, Apollos, nor any other
person is the unique center among the believers. This center is
not even a narrow Christ, the Christ of your preference. The

Christ who is the unique center of all believers is the One who is both theirs and ours." If we see this, we shall care for Christ as the unique center of all the believers.

Again and again I would emphasize the fact that the unique center is Christ and Christ alone. Whether the church in your locality is good or bad, high or low, does not matter. What matters is Christ as the unique center. We all have been called into Him, called into the fellowship, the enjoyment, the participation, in Him. We have been called into a mutuality in which we are one with Him. Only this can swallow up divisions and eliminate all the differences and preferences among the saints.

Consider the situation among Christians today: there is preference after preference. Some prefer to be Presbyterians, whereas others prefer to be Baptists, Methodists, Lutherans, or Pentecostals. Some say, "I like this," and others say, "I like that." Some declare, "I like this pastor," and others say, "I like that minister." "I like...I like," is commonly uttered by believers today. You may like a certain thing, but God may not like it. God is only pleased with Christ. God has one center—Jesus Christ—and He has called you not into the denomination of your choice, but into the fellowship of His Son. No individual or group must be our preference. Our only preference, our one choice, must be Christ as the unique center, the Christ who is theirs and ours, the Christ into whose mutuality we have been called by God. Oh, we all must see that God has called us into the fellowship of such a Christ!

In 1:10 Paul begins to deal with the divisions among the Corinthians. First, he beseeches them through the name of the Lord, which is the name above all names (Phil. 2:9) and should be the unique name among all His believers....To keep the oneness in the Lord and to avoid divisions, we need to uplift and exalt the unique name of our Lord by dropping all names other than this highest name. (*Life-study of 1 Corinthians,* pp. 26-27, 30)

Further Reading: Life-study of 1 Corinthians, msgs. 3-4, 14

Enlightenment and inspiration: _____

_____

_____

_____

Morning Nourishment

1 Cor. 1:10 Now I beseech you, brothers, through the name of our Lord Jesus Christ, that you all speak the same thing and *that* there be no divisions among you, but *that* you be attuned in the same mind and in the same opinion.

Col. 3:11 Where there cannot be Greek and Jew, circumcision and uncircumcision, barbarian, Scythian, slave, free man, but Christ is all and in all.

Phil. 2:2 Make my joy full, that you think the same thing, having the same love, joined in soul, thinking the one thing.

Rom. 15:6 That with one accord you may with one mouth glorify the God and Father of our Lord Jesus Christ.

In 1 Corinthians 1:10 Paul also tells the Corinthians to be "attuned in the same mind and in the same opinion." The Greek word rendered *attuned* here...means to repair, to restore, to adjust, to mend, making a broken thing thoroughly complete, joined perfectly together. The Corinthian believers as a whole were divided; their oneness was broken. They needed mending to join them perfectly together that they might be in harmony, having the same mind and the same opinion to speak the same thing, that is, Christ and His cross.

The testimony of the church in Corinth had been severely damaged, and Paul wrote this Epistle to mend this situation. This mending was also an attuning. The word *attune* is a musical term. Among the saints in Corinth there was no harmony. In writing this Epistle Paul was seeking to restore the harmony, to attune them so that they might be attuned in the same mind and in the same opinion. (*Life-study of 1 Corinthians,* p. 55)

Today's Reading

The problem among the Corinthians was not with their spirit. They had been regenerated, and the Lord Jesus dwelt in their spirit. Their problems were with the mind and their opinions....Thinking takes place in the mind; opinions are thoughts expressed in words....To be attuned to the same opinion actually means to speak the same thing. When we all speak the same thing, we are in the same opinion.

If we would be attuned in the same opinion, we need to have a vision of the place of Christ in God's economy. I am burdened that all the saints would see Christ and know Him. When you have seen the all-inclusive Christ and have learned the secret of enjoying Him, your way of thinking and speaking will be changed. Then you will become pure and simple. Instead of expressing your own opinions, you will care only to enjoy Christ and speak of Him. Having become a person who does not know anything except Christ, you will be faithful to the Lord's recovery.

Today the Lord is seeking a people who care only for Him. Collectively, here and there, these people will be lampstands. Among them, there will be no preferences or opinions—only Christ. May we all learn this secret.

Suppose you come into the meeting hall and the chairs are arranged in a very unusual way, altogether contrary to your preference. It should not make any difference to us how the chairs are arranged. As long as we can meet together to read the Word and speak of Christ, we should be satisfied. If you complain about the arrangement of the chairs and are distracted by it, this proves that you have not seen the vision concerning Christ....In the Lord's recovery we care only for Christ. In the recovery the Lord is not recovering anything other than Christ Himself in our experience. Only by focusing on Christ can we be saved from division.

By nature we all are divisive. We were born with a divisive element. The only way to be rescued from this divisiveness is to see the all-inclusive Christ and learn the secret of enjoying Him. Please be impressed that the only way to avoid division is to see Christ, receive Christ, and enjoy Christ. This and only this will cause us to be attuned in the same opinion. Then there will be real harmony among us. (*Life-study of 1 Corinthians,* pp. 55-57)

Further Reading: Life-study of 1 Corinthians, msg. 6

Enlightenment and inspiration: _____

_____
_____
_____

Hymns, #501

1   O glorious Christ, Savior mine,
Thou art truly radiance divine;
God infinite, in eternity,
Yet man in time, finite to be.

    Oh! Christ, expression of God, the Great,
Inexhaustible, rich, and sweet!
God mingled with humanity
Lives in me my all to be.

2   The fulness of God dwells in Thee;
Thou dost manifest God's glory;
In flesh Thou hast redemption wrought;
As Spirit, oneness with me sought.

3   All things of the Father are Thine;
All Thou art in Spirit is mine;
The Spirit makes Thee real to me,
That Thou experienced might be.

4   The Spirit of life causes Thee
By Thy Word to transfer to me.
Thy Spirit touched, Thy word received,
Thy life in me is thus conceived.

5   In spirit while gazing on Thee,
As a glass reflecting Thy glory,
Like to Thyself transformed I'll be,
That Thou might be expressed thru me.

6   In no other way could we be
Sanctified and share Thy vict'ry;
Thus only spiritual we'll be
And touch the life of glory.

7   Thy Spirit will me saturate,
Every part will God permeate,
Deliv'ring me from the old man,
With all saints building for His plan.

*Composition for prophecy with main point and
sub-points:* _____

_____

_____

_____

_____

_____

_____

_____

_____

_____

_____

_____

_____

_____

_____

_____

_____

_____

_____

_____

_____

_____

_____

_____

_____

_____

_____

_____

_____

_____

_____

_____

_____

_____

_____

Enjoying the Crucified Christ as the Unique Solution to All Problems in the Church

Scripture Reading: 1 Cor. 1:23-24, 30;2:2, 9-10; 5:7-8; 10:4; 15:45b; 1 Pet. 2:24

Day 1 I. **The crucified Christ was the unique subject, the center, the content, and the substance of the apostle's ministry (1 Cor. 2:2):**

A. The death of Christ has become God's power to eliminate all the problems in the universe; thus, Christ crucified is God's power to abolish all negative things and carry out His plan (1:23-24):

1. The human way of solving problems is to negotiate, but God's way is to terminate; the best way to solve problems among people is to terminate everyone involved (Gal. 2:20; cf. 1 Cor. 6:7-8).

2. The crucifixion of Christ has silenced the entire universe and simplified the extremely complicated situation in the universe (cf. 2 Cor. 11:2-3).

B. When we enjoy the crucified Christ, all that we are, all that we have, and all that we can do are completely terminated, and His resurrection life is imparted through us into others (John 12:24-26; 2 Cor. 4:10-12).

Day 2 II. **The enjoyment of the crucified Christ as the life-giving Spirit in our spirit solves all the problems in the church and issues in the growth in life for the building up of the church (1 Cor. 1:23; 2:2; 15:45b; 6:17; 3:6):**

A. The crucified Christ is the unleavened bread to be a feast to us (5:6-8):

1. Leaven signifies evil things and evil doctrines (vv. 6, 8; Matt. 16:6, 11-12); since Christ is unleavened, if we feast on Him daily, we can have an unleavened church life.

2. We need to enjoy Christ as our unleavened banquet for the entire period of our Christian life (1 Cor. 5:7-8; Exo. 12:15-20; cf. 13:4-9):

  a. The crucified Christ whom we enjoy today as our feast is the all-inclusive life-giving Spirit, and included in His being is His killing death; as long as we enjoy Him, we will be nourished, and the negative elements within us will be killed (1 Cor. 15:45b; Exo. 30:23-25).

  b. To eat the Lord Jesus, to feast on Him, is to receive Him into us that He may be assimilated by the regenerated new man in the way of life; we can eat Him by eating His words (John 6:57, 63; Jer. 15:16).

B. The crucified Christ is our spiritual rock who was smitten and cleft by God to flow Himself out as the spiritual water for us to drink (1 Cor. 10:4; John 19:34; Exo. 17:6):

1. We need to call on the Lord continually and draw water with joy from Him as the fountain of living water (1 Cor. 12:13, 3b; Isa. 12:3-4; John 4:10, 14).

2. We need to speak to the Lord constantly to receive Him as the living water (Num. 20:8).

Day 3
C. The crucified Christ is the power of God for us to live in any kind of environment and to live out every kind of virtue (1 Cor. 1:18, 24; Eph. 1:19-23):

1. We are able to live a contented life in any kind of environment by Christ as our inward power (Phil. 4:11-13).

2. We are able to live Christ out as every kind of virtue by Him as our inward power; to live a life of these virtues is much more difficult than doing a Christian work (vv. 13, 8).

3. We can enjoy the transmission of Christ as the power of God and the transfusion of Christ as the peace of God by practicing fellowship with Him in prayer (vv. 6-7).

Day 4

D. The crucified Christ is the wisdom of God as righteousness, sanctification, and redemption to us (1 Cor. 1:30):

   1. Christ became wisdom to us from God to transmit all that He is into our tripartite being for His eternal expression, making us the masterpiece of God for the wise exhibition of all that Christ is (Eph. 2:10; 3:10):

      a. Christ is our righteousness (for our past), by which we have been justified by God, that we might be reborn in our spirit to receive the divine life (Rom. 5:18; 8:10).

      b. Christ is our sanctification (for our present), by which we are being sanctified in our soul—transformed in our mind, emotion, and will—with His divine life (6:19, 22).

      c. Christ is our redemption (for our future), the redemption of our body, by which we will be transfigured in our body with His divine life to have His glorious likeness (8:23; Phil. 3:21).

      d. It is of God that we participate in such a complete and perfect salvation, which makes our entire being—spirit, soul, and body—organically one with Christ and makes Christ everything to us (cf. Eph. 5:25-27).

   2. Righteousness, sanctification, and redemption refer not only to three stages of God's salvation but also to three aspects of the nature of God's salvation that we need to experience daily.

   3. When we lay hold of Christ as the personified wisdom of God, He becomes the reality of the tree of life to us for us to minister Christ as life to others (Prov. 3:18-19; 2 Chron. 1:10; Col. 2:2-3; 1:28; 1 Tim. 5:1-2).

Day 5

E. The crucified Christ is our Healer, our healing tree (Exo. 15:22-26; 1 Pet. 2:24; John 11:25; Rev. 2:7):
1. When we experience the healing tree of the cross of Christ and live a crucified life, our bitter situation becomes sweet.
2. We need to apply the cross of Christ to our whole being, that the bitterness within us may be healed and changed into sweetness.

Day 6

F. The crucified Christ is the depths, the deep things, of God (1 Cor. 2:6-10):
1. The deep things of God are Christ in many aspects as our eternal portion, foreordained, prepared, and given to us freely by God (Rom. 11:33; 1 Cor. 15:45b; 6:17).
2. To realize and participate in the deep and hidden things God has ordained and prepared for us requires us to love Him (2:9; Mark 12:30; cf. 1 Cor. 16:22):
   a. In this way we have the closest and most intimate fellowship with God, and we are able to enter into His heart and apprehend all its secrets (Psa. 73:25; 25:14).
   b. When our entire being becomes one with God through loving Him in intimate fellowship, He shows us, in our spirit through His Spirit, all the secrets of Christ as our portion (1 Cor. 2:10-12).

Morning Nourishment

1 Cor. **For I did not determine to know anything among**
2:2 **you except Jesus Christ, and this One crucified.**
1:23 **But we preach Christ crucified, to Jews a stum-**
bling block, and to Gentiles foolishness.
Gal. **I am crucified with Christ; and *it is* no longer I**
2:20 ***who* live, but *it is* Christ *who* lives in me; and the**
***life* which I now live in the flesh I live in faith,**
the *faith* of the Son of God, who loved me and
gave Himself up for me.

When we experience the crucified Christ, we are terminated.
All that we are, all that we have, and all that we can do—all is
completely terminated. To be terminated, there is no need for
you to crucify yourself. There is not even any need for you to
reckon yourself dead. You are terminated simply by experiencing the crucified Christ. Actually, it is impossible for anyone to
crucify himself. But when we call on the name of the Lord Jesus,
as we are enjoying Him and experiencing Him, His crucifixion
will terminate us. All that we are is terminated by this crucified
Christ. (*Life-study of 1 Corinthians,* p. 76)

Today's Reading

The first two chapters of 1 Corinthians are very difficult to
understand....The main point in these chapters is that in his
spirit Paul was endeavoring to bring the distracted philosophical believers back to Christ. For this reason, in these chapters
Paul does not emphasize the resurrected Christ or the ascended
Christ; instead, he emphasizes the crucified Christ. In 2:2 he
says, "I did not determine to know anything among you except
Jesus Christ, and this One crucified." To the Corinthians Paul
proclaimed a crucified Christ, a Christ who had been killed.

We have pointed out that the best way to solve problems
among people is to terminate everyone involved. However, the
human way of solving problems is to negotiate. God's way, on
the contrary, is not to negotiate, but to terminate. When everyone has been terminated, there is silence. The best way to bring

in silence and simplicity is to have a Christ who has been crucified. It seems as if Paul was saying to the Corinthians, "I testified to you a Christ who had been crucified. When I first came to you, I preached to you concerning the crucified Christ. The Lord's life on earth ended with death by crucifixion."

The fact that Christ was crucified implies many things. It implies that He was despised, rejected, and defeated. No one could be crucified without first being rejected and defeated. Through crucifixion Christ suffered man's rejection. He was able to avoid death by crucifixion, but He did not do so. He could be crucified only because He was willing to be killed. The crucifixion of Christ has silenced the entire universe and simplified the extremely complicated situation in the universe.

Deep in his spirit, Paul was yearning to impress the distracted, philosophical Christians in Corinth with this crucified Christ. Among the saints there was turmoil and trouble. Many voices were speaking different things: "I am of Apollos," "I am of Cephas," "I am of Paul," "I am of Christ." What could silence all these voices? Paul knew that they could be silenced only by a crucified Christ. Therefore, in Paul's spirit was the burden to bring the believers back to the Christ whom he had preached to them and testified to them. Paul could say, "The Christ I preached to you was a silent Christ, a Christ who was willing to be crucified without a word. He was willing to be despised, rejected, and put to death. This is the Christ I ministered to you when I came to you. Now I want you to know that such a Christ is God's power. Only a crucified Christ can save you. God's saving power is not a strong Christ but a crucified Christ, not a fighting Christ but a defeated Christ." I repeat, Paul's spirit was to bring back these striving, philosophical Christians to the simplicity and silence of the crucified Christ. (*Life-study of 1 Corinthians*, pp. 60-62)

Further Reading: Life-study of 1 Corinthians, msgs. 5-8, 15;
   The Excelling Gift for the Building Up of the Church, ch. 1

Enlightenment and inspiration: _____

_____

_____

_____

Morning Nourishment

1 Cor. **Purge out the old leaven that you may be a new**
5:7-8 **lump, even as you are unleavened; for our Passover, Christ, also has been sacrificed. So then let
us keep the feast, not with old leaven, neither
with the leaven of malice and evil, but with the
unleavened *bread* of sincerity and truth.**
10:3-4 **And all ate the same spiritual food, and all drank
the same spiritual drink; for they drank of a
spiritual rock which followed *them*, and the rock
was Christ.**

In chapter five of 1 Corinthians, Christ is our Passover and our unleavened bread for us to keep the feast (vv. 7-8). A feast is altogether an enjoyment. In chapter ten Christ is our spiritual food and our spiritual drink (vv. 3-4), and He gave Himself to us by being crucified so that we can enjoy the fellowship of His blood and body (v. 16). In this Christ there is an absolute, wonderful, excellent, and killing death. In the crucified and resurrected Christ, there is the killing element that kills all of our negative "germs." The food that we eat every day, on the one hand, nourishes us, and on the other hand, kills the negative elements in our physical body. In like manner, if we eat Christ every day to enjoy Him, we will be nourished and the negative elements within us will be killed.

The enjoyment of the all-inclusive Christ solves the problems in the church through the work of the cross (1:13a, 18, 23-24; 2:2). By "the cross" I mean the death of Christ, especially the subjective aspect of His death. The Christ that we enjoy today is the all-inclusive One, and included in His being is the killing death....Because there were so many problems among the Corinthians, Paul wrote to them concerning the enjoyment of Christ. This enjoyment solves our problems by killing the germs within us. (*The Excelling Gift for the Building Up of the Church*, p. 11)

Today's Reading

In...1 Corinthians Paul compares the believers at Corinth, and himself as well, to the children of Israel....This gives us the ground to say that the history of the children of Israel is a full type of our Christian life in the church. In 5:7 Paul speaks of "our Passover, Christ." If Christ was Paul's Passover, then He must be the Passover for every believer. The children of Israel did not live individualistically....Their corporate life typifies our life in the church....What happened to them is a type of our experience today. They ate manna in the wilderness; we also eat manna. They drank of the living water; we also drink the living water. They had a rock which went with them; we also have a rock. They experienced the Passover; we also have a Passover,...Christ Himself. Furthermore, after the Passover, they kept the feast of unleavened bread. This indicates that we also should keep this feast. The church life is a feast of unleavened bread. For this reason, any leaven must be purged out of the church.

Unleavened bread indicates a living which is without sin, without leaven. In ourselves we cannot possibly have this kind of living. However, in Christ it is possible to live a sinless life. We have been put into Christ, and now we must learn to live in Christ and by Christ. Then He will become our unleavened life supply. He will become the source, the fountain, of a sinless life and living. Because we have such a source and supply, it is possible for us to live a sinless life.

If we would live a life without sin, we must daily eat Christ as unleavened bread. Dietitians tell us that we are what we eat. If we eat unleavened bread, we shall eventually become constituted of unleavened bread. Then we shall live an unleavened life. Although in ourselves it is impossible ever to be sinless, in Christ we can become sinless by eating Him as the source and supply of a sinless life. Since Christ, our source, is unleavened, if we feast on Him daily, we can have an unleavened church life. (*Life-study of 1 Corinthians*, pp. 323-324)

Further Reading: The Excelling Gift for the Building Up of the Church, ch. 1; *Life-study of 1 Corinthians*, msg. 36; *The Crucial Revelation of Life in the Scriptures*, ch. 4; *Life-study of Proverbs*, msg. 6

Enlightenment and inspiration: _____
_____
_____
_____

Morning Nourishment

1 Cor. For the word of the cross is to those who are
 1:18 perishing foolishness, but to us who are being
      saved it is the power of God.
   24 But to those who are called, both Jews and Greeks,
      Christ the power of God and the wisdom of God.
Phil. Finally, brothers, what things are true, what
 4:8 things are dignified, what things are righteous,
      what things are pure, what things are lovely, what
      things are well spoken of, if there is any virtue and
      if any praise, take account of these things.
   13 I am able to do all things in Him who empowers me.

In the cross of Christ we see God's power. It takes the power
of God to defeat Satan, the world, sin, fallen man, the flesh, the
natural life, the old creation, and the ordinances. What other power
is greater than Christ crucified as God's power? What other power
can destroy Satan or overcome the world? Only God has the
power to accomplish these things. This power is not that of doing
things by speaking, such as the power God exercised in creation.
Rather, it is the power of crucifixion, the power of the wonderful
death of Christ. This means that the crucifixion of Christ has
become the power of God. The death of Christ has become God's
power to destroy Satan, to solve the problem of the world, to
eliminate sin, and to terminate fallen man, the flesh, the natural
life, and the old creation. By this power God is able also to solve
the problem of the ordinances. By one death, the death of Christ,
all the problems in the universe have been cleared. Thus, Christ
crucified is God's power to abolish all negative things and carry
out His plan. (*Life-study of 1 Corinthians,* p. 73)

Today's Reading

Christ lives in the believers for them to be able to do all things
in Him who empowers them. Paul says, "I am able to do all
things in Him who empowers me" (Phil. 4:13). To be empowered
by Christ is to be made dynamic inwardly. Christ dwells in us
(Col. 1:27), and He empowers us, makes us dynamic, from

within, not from without. By such inward empowering, Paul could do all things in Christ.

Paul was a person in Christ (2 Cor. 12:2) and he desired to be found in Christ by others (Phil. 3:9). In 4:13 he declared that he could do all things in Christ, the One who empowered him. This is an all-inclusive and concluding word of Paul's experience of Christ....As long as we have Christ and are in Him, we can do all things in Him.

In Philippians 4:13 we find the secret to which Paul refers in verse 12, "The secret both to be filled and to hunger, both to abound and to lack." In chapter three Paul testified that he pursued Christ in order to gain Him and be found in Him. Now in 4:13 Paul says that he is in Him. In Christ as the One who empowers him Paul could do all things. Christ was his secret of sufficiency. By being in Him Paul could do all things in Him.

The "all things" in Philippians 4:13 refer to the things mentioned in verse 12 and to the virtues listed in verse 8. This means that the application of verse 13 is limited by the context of verses 8 through 13. By the empowering of Christ we can live a contented life (vv. 11-12) and be true, dignified, righteous, pure, lovely, and well spoken of. This means that we are persons in Christ, who empowers us to live out every kind of virtue. This is to live Christ, to magnify Christ in His virtues.

To live a life of all these virtues is much more difficult than doing a Christian work. Many can preach the gospel, teach the Bible, and even establish churches, but they are not able to live this kind of life, a life full of the virtues of being true, dignified, righteous, pure, lovely, and well spoken of. In order to live Christ as our human virtues for the expression of the divine attributes, we need to be empowered by the indwelling Christ. (*The Conclusion of the New Testament,* pp. 1554-1555)

Further Reading: Life-study of 1 Corinthians, msg. 8; *The Conclusion of the New Testament,* msg. 143

Enlightenment and inspiration: _____
_____
_____
_____

Morning Nourishment

1 Cor. **But of Him you are in Christ Jesus, who became**
1:30 **wisdom to us from God: both righteousness and sanctification and redemption.**

Rom. **But if Christ is in you,...the spirit is life because**
8:10 **of righteousness.**

6:22 **But now, having been freed from sin and enslaved to God, you have your fruit unto sanctification, and the end, eternal life.**

8:23 **...We...who have the firstfruits of the Spirit, even we ourselves groan in ourselves, eagerly awaiting sonship, the redemption of our body.**

In 1 Corinthians 1:30...Paul does not say that Christ *is* wisdom to us; he says that Christ *became* wisdom to us. This indicates that at one time Christ was not wisdom to us, but that He later became wisdom to us....Christ could not become wisdom to us before we were in Him. But when we believed in Christ, God put us into Him. Then Christ became wisdom to us.

Christ became wisdom "to us from God." The expression *to us from God* indicates something present, practical, and experiential in the way of transmission. Continually, Christ must become wisdom to us from God. This indicates a living, ongoing transmission. The words *to* and *from* indicate that a present, living, and practical transmission is taking place from God to us.

Paul composed verse 30 in the way he did in order to indicate to the believers in Corinth that Christ should continually become wisdom to them from God. Christ as wisdom should unceasingly flow from God to them. However, their actual situation was contrary to this. Christ may have been their wisdom, but He was not presently flowing to them from God. Once again I wish to point out that Paul does not say, "Christ is God's wisdom," or "Christ is your wisdom." He says, "Christ became wisdom to us from God." This indicates that Christ should continually flow from God to us and be our present and practical wisdom in our experience. (*Life-study of 1 Corinthians,* pp. 83-84)

Today's Reading

Christ was made wisdom to us from God as three vital things in God's salvation: righteousness (for our past), by which we have been justified by God, that we might be reborn in our spirit to receive the divine life (Rom. 5:18); sanctification (for the present), by which we are being sanctified in our soul, that is, transformed in our mind, emotion, and will, with the divine life (Rom. 6:19, 22); and redemption (for the future), that is, the redemption of our body (Rom. 8:23), by which we will be transfigured in our body with His divine life to have His glorious likeness (Phil. 3:21). It is of God that we participate in such a complete and perfect salvation, making our entire being—spirit, soul, and body—organically one with Christ, and making Christ everything to us. It is altogether of God, not of ourselves, that we may boast and glory in Him, not in ourselves.

Righteousness, sanctification, and redemption are not only related to our past, present, and future. Daily we need Christ as righteousness, sanctification, and redemption.

Redemption includes three matters: termination, replacement, and being brought back to God. When God redeems us, He terminates us, replaces us with Christ, and brings us back to Himself.

In the church life we...need redemption because in many matters we are still very natural....Thus, in the church life we need to be terminated, replaced with Christ, and brought back to God. In all things we need to be righteous, sanctified, and redeemed. When Christ becomes wisdom to us from God, eventually in everything He will be our righteousness, sanctification, and redemption. How deep and profound is Paul's thought here! (*Life-study of 1 Corinthians,* pp. 84-86)

Further Reading: Life-study of 1 Corinthians, msg. 9; *The Advance of the Lord's Recovery Today,* ch. 4; *Life-study of Proverbs,* msg. 2; *The Divine Dispensing of the Divine Trinity,* ch. 25

Enlightenment and inspiration: _____

_____

_____

Morning Nourishment

Exo.   **And when they came to Marah, they could not**
15:23 **drink of the waters of Marah, for they were bitter;**
       therefore its name was called Marah.
25-26 **And he cried out to Jehovah, and Jehovah showed**
       him a tree; and he cast it into the waters, and the
       waters became sweet. There He made for them a
       statute and an ordinance, and there He tested
       them. And He said,...I am Jehovah who heals you.
1 Pet. **Who Himself bore up our sins in His body on the**
2:24   **tree, in order that we, having died to sins, might live**
       to righteousness; by whose bruise you were healed.

When I have been in bitter circumstances, often the Lord has
pointed me to the cross of Christ. I realized that I needed to take
the cross and live a crucified life. This saved me from my bitter
situation, and my bitter circumstances were healed. However,
at the same time the Lord has often shown me that there is
bitterness within me. I saw that there was bitterness in my self
as well as in my circumstances. I also saw that there is bitterness
in my whole being, in my spirit, soul, and body, and that I needed
to apply the cross of Christ to every aspect of my being. Spiritually,
psychologically, and physically I needed the application of the
cross of Christ. Time and time again I have experienced the Lord's
healing in this way. As my situation was healed, I was healed
inwardly. Both in my circumstances and in my being, bitterness
was changed into sweetness. (*Life-study of Exodus,* p. 352)

Today's Reading

God led the people to Marah, which means bitterness....The
pillar of cloud led the people to a place where there were waters,
but these waters were bitter. When the people discovered that the
waters were bitter, they "murmured against Moses, saying, What
shall we drink?" (Exo. 15:24). Like the children of Israel, we also
have complained and murmured about our bitter situations....As
a true servant of the Lord, instead of striving with this murmur-
ing and complaining people, Moses cried out to the Lord (v. 25).

In response to his cry, the Lord showed him a tree (v. 25). When Moses cast the tree into the waters, the waters were made sweet. First Peter 2:24 indicates that this tree signifies the cross of Christ. Thus, the tree that healed the bitter waters denotes the cross on which the Lord was crucified. The cross of Christ, the unique cross, is the healing cross.

This picture corresponds to our spiritual experience. After we are baptized and begin to walk in newness of life, we are troubled because we have no natural water. On the one hand, we are like the people who complained and murmured. On the other hand, we are like Moses who cried to the Lord. When we cry out to the Lord in prayer, He shows us the vision of the crucified Christ.... Seeing this vision, we apply the cross of Christ to our situation, and immediately the bitter waters become sweet.

The Lord's word in Exodus 15:26 indicates that in His eyes the children of Israel were sick and in need of healing....The same is true of us today. In certain parts of our inward being we are still sick and need the Lord's healing....The process of healing takes place as we are touched by the cross of Christ. The only way to be touched by the cross is to see the vision of the tree and to cast this tree into the very place that needs to be healed. If your mind is bitter, cast the tree into your mind. If your attitude toward some one or some thing is bitter, cast the tree into your attitude. Do this with every part of your being, and little by little you will be healed. Every time we experience the cross of Christ, we shall have a deeper realization of our need to be healed through the touch of the cross. We need to be identified with the crucifixion of Christ by applying His cross to every part of our being that is bitter and sick. Then those parts will be healed. In this way daily and even hourly the Lord Jesus becomes our Healer. (*Life-study of Exodus*, pp. 349-350, 355)

Further Reading: Life-study of Exodus, msg. 30; *The Crucial Revelation of Life in the Scriptures,* ch. 4*

Enlightenment and inspiration: _____

_____

_____

_____

Morning Nourishment

1 Cor. But as it is written, "Things which eye has not seen
2:9-10 and ear has not heard and *which* have not come
     up in man's heart; things which God has prepared
     for those who love Him." But to us God has re-
     vealed *them* through the Spirit, for the Spirit
     searches all things, even the depths of God.

Psa. Whom do I have in heaven *but You?* And besides
73:25 You there is nothing I desire on earth.

25:14 The intimate counsel of Jehovah is to those who fear
     Him, and His covenant will He make known to them.

To realize and participate in the deep and hidden things God
has ordained and prepared for us [1 Cor. 2:9] requires us not
only to believe in Him, but also to love Him. To fear God, to
worship God, and to believe in God, that is, to receive God, are
all inadequate; to love Him is the indispensable requirement.
To love God means to set our entire being—spirit, soul, and body,
with the heart, soul, mind, and strength (Mark 12:30)—absolutely on Him, that is, to let our entire being be occupied by Him
and lost in Him, so that He becomes everything to us and we
are one with Him practically in our daily life. In this way we
have the closest and most intimate fellowship with God. It is
thus we are able to enter into His heart and apprehend all its
secrets (Psa. 73:25; 25:14). Thus, we not only realize, but also
experience, enjoy, and fully participate in these deep and hidden
things of God. (*Life-study of 1 Corinthians,* p. 144)

Today's Reading

In 1 Corinthians 2:6 Paul says that the wisdom we speak is
not a wisdom of this age nor of the rulers of this age. In
themselves, human beings are not capable of knowing this
wisdom. It must be revealed through the Spirit....God reveals
the deep and hidden things to us through the Spirit [v. 10], for
these things have not been seen by man's eyes, heard by man's
ears, nor have they come up in man's heart. This means that
man has no idea concerning them, no thought of them. They are

altogether mysterious, hidden in God, and beyond human understanding. But God has revealed them to us through the Spirit, who searches all things, even the depths of God.

To have something revealed to us is different from being taught about that thing. To teach is related to our mind; to reveal, to our spirit. To realize the deep and hidden things God has prepared for us, our spirit is more necessary than our mind. When our entire being becomes one with God through loving Him in intimate fellowship, He shows us, in our spirit through His Spirit, all the secrets of Christ as our portion. This is to reveal the hidden things planned by His wisdom concerning Christ, things which have never come up in man's heart.

First Corinthians 2:10 says that the Spirit searches all things....The Spirit of God explores the depths of God concerning Christ and shows them to us in our spirit for our realization and participation.

The depths of God refer to the deep things of God, which are Christ in many aspects as our eternal portion, foreordained, prepared, and given to us freely by God. These...are revealed to us in our spirit by God's Spirit. Hence, we must be spiritual in order to partake of them. We must move and live in our spirit that we may enjoy Christ as everything to us.

To know the depths of God is to know Christ in many aspects as our eternal portion. Christ is the center of God's economy, the portion given to us by God for our enjoyment, and the mysterious wisdom hidden in God. God's wisdom in a mystery is Christ as the deep things of God. I encourage you all to pray and fellowship concerning this and to seek a deeper understanding of the depths of God—Christ Himself as the mysterious and hidden wisdom, the focus of God's economy, and the portion given to us by God for our enjoyment. Christ, the all-inclusive and extensive One, is truly the depths of God. (*Life-study of 1 Corinthians,* pp. 145, 147)

Further Reading: Life-study of 1 Corinthians, msg. 16; *The Conclusion of the New Testament,* msg. 56

Enlightenment and inspiration: _____

_____

_____

_____

Hymns, #477

1 Though Christ a thousand times
  In Bethlehem be born,
  If He's not born in thee
  Thy soul is still forlorn.
  The Cross on Golgotha,
  Will never save thy soul;
  The Cross in thine own heart,
  Alone can make thee whole.

  O, Cross of Christ, I take thee
    Into this heart of mine,
  That I to my own self may die
    And rise to thy life Divine.

2 What e'er thou lovest, man,
  That too become thou must;
  God, if thou lovest God,
  Dust, if thou lovest dust.
  Go out, God will come in;
  Die thou and let Him live;
  Be not and He will be;
  Wait and He'll all things give.

3 To bring thee to thy God,
  Love takes the shortest route;
  The way which knowledge leads,
  Is but a roundabout.
  Drive out from thee the world,
  And then thy heart shall be
  Filled with the love of God,
  And holy like as He.

Composition for prophecy with main point and sub-points: _____

_____
_____
_____
_____
_____
_____
_____
_____
_____
_____
_____
_____
_____
_____
_____
_____
_____
_____
_____
_____
_____
_____
_____
_____
_____
_____
_____
_____
_____
_____
_____
_____
_____
_____
_____
_____

The Goal of 1 Corinthians

Scripture Reading: 1 Cor. 2:10-16; 3:1, 3, 16; 14:32, 37; 4:1

Day 1

I. **The goal of 1 Corinthians was to motivate the Corinthian believers who were soulish, fleshy, and fleshly to aspire to the growth in life that they might become spiritual men for God's building (2:15; 3:1, 3; 14:32, 37):**

A. First Corinthians reveals that a believer may be one of three kinds of men:

1. A believer may be a spiritual man, living in his spirit under the anointing of the Holy Spirit (Rom. 8:4; Gal. 5:25; 1 Cor. 15:45b; 6:17):

   a. A spiritual man is one who does not behave according to the flesh or act according to the soulish life but lives according to the spirit, that is, his spirit mingled with the Spirit of God; such a man is ruled and controlled by his spirit (2:15).

   b. A spiritual man denies his soul and does not live by his soul but allows his spirit, that is, his regenerated spirit, which is occupied and energized by the Spirit of God, to dominate his entire being.

   c. A spiritual man is dominated, governed, directed, moved, and led by his mingled spirit (5:3-5a; 6:17; 2 Cor. 2:13-14).

2. A believer may be a soulish man, living in his soul under the direction of the soul, the natural life (1 Cor. 2:14):

   a. A soulish man is a natural man, one who allows his soul (including the mind, the emotion, and the will) to dominate his entire being and who lives by his soul, ignoring his spirit, not using his spirit, and even behaving as if he did not have a spirit (Jude 19).

b. Such a man does not receive the things of
the Spirit of God, and he is not able to
know them; to such natural men the
things of the Spirit of God are foolishness
(1 Cor. 1:22-23).

3. A believer may be a fleshy and fleshly man,
being of the flesh and living in the flesh under
the influence of the nature of the flesh (3:1, 3):

a. *Fleshy* denotes being made of flesh;
fleshly denotes being influenced by the
nature of the flesh and partaking of the
character of the flesh.

b. The jealousy and strife among the Corinthian believers show that they walked
according to the flesh of the fallen man
and not according to the human spirit
regenerated by God (vv. 3-4; 1:11-12; Gal.
5:19-21).

4. The Lord desires that all His believers take
His grace to be the first kind of man—a
spiritual man (6:18; Rev. 22:21).

5. As we have been called by God into the
fellowship of Christ (1 Cor. 1:9), who is now
the life-giving Spirit (15:45b), and as we are
one spirit with Him (6:17), we can experience
and enjoy Him only when we live in our spirit
under the leading of the Holy Spirit.

Day 2 B. Our spirit is typified by the Holy of Holies and
the good land; we must live and serve in our
spirit for God's building (John 4:24; 1 Cor. 14:32;
Rom. 1:9):

1. We are the temple of God, and the three parts
of our being correspond to the three parts of
the temple: our body corresponds to the outer
court, our soul to the Holy Place, and our
spirit to the Holy of Holies, which is the very
residence of Christ as the life-giving Spirit,
who is the presence of the Triune God (1 Cor.
3:16; 2 Tim. 4:22; John 14:16-20).

2. The three parts of our being also correspond
to the three places of Israel's journey: Egypt
corresponds to the flesh (our fallen body), the
wilderness to our soul, and the good land to
our spirit where Christ as the reality of the
good land dwells:

   a. The all-inclusive Christ as the life-giving
   Spirit is the reality of the good land in our
   spirit, making our mingled spirit the land
   of Immanuel (Gal. 3:14; Matt. 1:23; 2 Tim.
   4:22; Isa. 8:7-8, 10).

   b. In 1 Corinthians Paul likened the Corinthians to the children of Israel, who experienced Christ as the Passover in Egypt
   (5:7) and who wandered in the wilderness,
   experiencing Christ as the heavenly
   manna and as the spiritual rock which
   flowed out the living water (10:3-4).

   c. The record of entering into the good land
   is in 2 Corinthians, which is an autobiography of a person in the spirit; the good
   land in 2 Corinthians is Christ Himself as
   the life-giving Spirit given to us as the
   divine grace in our spirit for our enjoyment (13:14; 12:9; cf. Heb. 10:29).

   d. Paul's burden is for us to enter into and
   enjoy the reality of the good land, the
   all-inclusive Christ as the life-giving
   Spirit of grace in our spirit, today's Holy
   of Holies, for God's building (2 Cor. 2:13;
   John 14:16-20; Heb. 9:3-4).

II. **The way to experience all the aspects of
Christ in 1 Corinthians for God's building is
through the two spirits, the divine Spirit and
the regenerated human spirit, mingled together as one spirit (2:10-16; John 3:6; 4:24;
Rom. 8:16; 1 Cor. 15:45b; 6:17):**

   A. Only the spirit of man can know the things of
   man; the things of man include man's position,

situation, condition, need, source, and destiny (cf. Mark 2:8a).

B. Only the Spirit of God can know the deep things of God (1 Cor. 2:10-11).

C. When we exercise our spirit to know the things of man, we are ushered into the Spirit of God to know Christ as the deep things of God; we must move, act, and live in our spirit that we may enjoy Christ as everything to us (vv. 9-10):

1. The Corinthian believers had neglected the spirit of man and the Spirit of God, having turned instead to live in their mind by philosophy.

2. Hence, 1 Corinthians shows that the proper experience of these two spirits is essential for the practice of the church life.

Day 6

D. A spiritual man is a steward of the mysteries of God (Christ as the mystery of God and the church as the mystery of Christ), a dispenser of the divine life supply to God's children for God's building (4:1; Col. 2:2; Eph. 3:4):

1. A spiritual man has the mind of Christ (1 Cor. 2:15-16).

2. A spiritual man speaks the spiritual things, which are the deep things of God concerning Christ, with spiritual words, which are words taught by the Spirit; furthermore, only a spiritual man can receive them; this divine speaking is prophesying for God's building (vv. 13-15; 14:4b, 31-32).

Morning Nourishment

1 Cor. 2:14-15	But a soulish man does not receive the things of the Spirit of God, for they are foolishness to him and he is not able to know *them* because they are discerned spiritually. But the spiritual man discerns all things, but he himself is discerned by no one.
3:1	And I, brothers, was not able to speak to you as to spiritual men, but as to fleshy, as to infants in Christ.
6:17	But he who is joined to the Lord is one spirit.
Gal. 5:25	If we live by the Spirit, let us also walk by the Spirit.

First Corinthians reveals clearly that a believer may be one of three kinds of men: a spiritual man, living in his spirit under the anointing of the Holy Spirit (Rom. 8:4; Gal. 5:25); a soulish man, living in his soul under the direction of the soul, the natural life (1 Cor. 2:14); or a fleshy and fleshly man, of the flesh and living in the flesh under the influence of the nature of the flesh. The Lord desires that all His believers may take His grace to be the first kind of man—a spiritual man. This is the goal of this book—to motivate the Corinthian believers who are soulish, fleshy, and fleshly to aspire to the growth in life that they may become spiritual (2:15; 3:1; 14:37). As we have been called by God into the fellowship of Christ (1:9), who is now the life-giving Spirit (15:45), and as we are one spirit with Him (6:17), we can experience and enjoy Him only when we live in our spirit under the leading of the Holy Spirit. When we live in the soul or in the flesh, we are missing the mark of participating in Him. (*Life-study of 1 Corinthians,* p. 212)

Today's Reading

In 1 Corinthians 3:1...Paul is very frank in telling the Corinthians that he could not speak unto them as to spiritual, but as to fleshy. A spiritual man is one who does not behave according to the flesh or act according to the soulish life, but lives according to the spirit, that is, his spirit mingled with the Spirit of God. Such a one is dominated, governed, directed, moved, and led by such a mingled spirit.

The term fleshy is a stronger expression than fleshly in verse 3, and it refers to aspects of the flesh that are more gross. Fleshy denotes made of flesh; fleshly denotes being influenced by the nature of the flesh, partaking of the character of the flesh. In verse 1 the apostle considers the Corinthian believers to be totally of the flesh....Then in verse 3 the apostle condemns their behaving in jealousy and strife as fleshly.

In 3:1 Paul refers to the believers at Corinth as infants in Christ. Although they had received all the initial gifts in life and were lacking in none of them (1:7), they had not grown in life after receiving them, but rather remained as infants in Christ, not spiritual but fleshy. The apostle here points out their deficiency and indicates their need, that is, to grow in life to maturity, to be full grown (2:6; Col. 1:28). In 1 Cor. 3:2 Paul goes on to say, "I gave you milk to drink, not solid food, for you were not yet able to receive it. But neither yet now are you able." To give milk to drink or food to eat is to feed others. Feeding refers to the matter of life. This differs from teaching, which refers to knowledge. What the apostle ministered to the Corinthian believers seemed to be knowledge. Actually it was milk (not yet solid food), and it should have nourished them. Milk is mainly for infants, whereas solid food is for the mature (Heb. 5:12). The fact that the Corinthian believers could not receive solid food indicates that they were not growing in life.

In 1 Corinthians 3:3 Paul continues, "For you are still fleshly. For if there is jealousy and strife among you, are you not fleshly and do you not walk according to the manner of man?" Jealousy and strife... characterize those who are in the flesh, those who are fleshly. Every fallen human being is the flesh (Rom. 3:20; Gal. 2:16). Therefore, to walk according to man is to walk according to the flesh. (*Life-study of 1 Corinthians,* pp. 211-213)

Further Reading: A General Sketch of the New Testament in the Light of Christ and the Church, chs. 12-13; *Life-study of 1 Corinthians,* msg. 24

Enlightenment and inspiration: _____

_____

_____

_____

Morning Nourishment

1 Cor. 3:16 Do you not know that you are the temple of God, and *that* the Spirit of God dwells in you?

2 Tim. 4:22 The Lord be with your spirit. Grace be with you.

Heb. 10:19 Having therefore, brothers, boldness for entering the *Holy of* Holies in the blood of Jesus.

God the Father is in us (Eph. 4:6), Christ is in us (2 Cor. 13:5), and the Holy Spirit is in us (Rom. 8:11). All three persons of the Triune God are in us. But where within us is the Triune God? In what part? It is so clear, beyond any ground of argument, that Christ today is in our spirit, and we have the Scriptures that confirm this fact. We should not be so vague, like many who say, "Oh, the Lord is in you and the Lord is in me." The last verse of 2 Timothy definitely states that Christ is in our spirit. "The Lord be with your spirit" (2 Tim. 4:22). In order for Christ to be in our spirit, He must first be Spirit; next, we must have a spirit; finally, these two spirits must be mingled as one spirit. If the Lord is not the Spirit, how could He be in our spirit, and how could we be one spirit with Him?

In order to locate the human spirit, we need to divide the soul from the spirit. "For the word of God is living and operative and sharper than any two-edged sword, and piercing even to the dividing of soul and spirit and of joints and marrow, and able to discern the thoughts and intentions of the heart" (Heb. 4:12). God's word is a sharp sword to pierce our being, to divide our soul from our spirit. (*The Economy of God,* pp. 27-28)

Today's Reading

We are told in 1 Corinthians 3 that we are the temple of God. God's temple according to the Old Testament is portrayed in three parts: the first is the outer court, the second is the Holy Place, and the third is the Holy of Holies, the most holy place.

We know that God was in His temple, but in what part? Was He in the outer court or in the Holy Place? No. He was in the Holy of Holies. There in the Holy of Holies dwelt the shekinah presence of God. In the outer court was the altar, which is a type of the cross, and directly behind the altar was the laver, which in type is the work of the Holy Spirit. The Holy Place included the showbread table, the lampstand, and the incense altar. But what was in the Holy of Holies? The ark which typifies Christ! Therefore, Christ was in the Holy of Holies, and God's presence, the shekinah glory of God, was there also.

The Scriptures point out that we too are the temple (1 Cor. 3:16). We as tripartite beings are also composed of three parts—the body, the soul, and the spirit. But in which part of our being does the Triune God dwell? Second Timothy 4:22 states clearly that the Lord is in our spirit. Our spirit is the very Holy of Holies. The typology of the Old Testament temple presents a very clear picture. Christ and God's presence are in the Holy of Holies. Today this type of the temple of God is fulfilled in us. We are of three parts: our body corresponds to the outer court, our soul to the Holy Place, and our human spirit to the Holy of Holies, which is the very residence of Christ and God's presence.

"Having therefore, brothers, boldness for entering the Holy of Holies in the blood of Jesus" (Heb. 10:19). What is "the Holy of Holies" for us to enter today while we are here on earth?…Our human spirit is the Holy of Holies which is God's residence, the very chamber in which God and Christ dwell. If we would find God and Christ, there is no need for us to go to heaven. God in Christ is so available, for He is in our spirit.

For this reason we have to divide our soul from our spirit (Heb. 4:12). If we are unable to divide the soul from the spirit, we simply cannot contact the Lord. Look at the picture. If the high priest was unable to locate the Holy of Holies, his efforts to contact God would only have ended in failure. First, he had to enter the outer court, and from the outer court he had to enter the Holy Place, and from the Holy Place he would finally enter the Holy of Holies. There he would meet God and see the shekinah glory of God's presence. (*The Economy of God,* pp. 28-30)

Further Reading: The Economy of God, ch. 3

Enlightenment and inspiration: _____

_____

_____

_____

Morning Nourishment

Gen. On that day Jehovah made a covenant with
15:18 Abram, saying, To your seed do I give this land...
Deut. And you shall do that which is right and good in
6:18 the sight of Jehovah so that it may go well with
you and you may enter and possess the good land,
concerning which Jehovah swore to your fathers.
Gal. In order that the blessing of Abraham might come
3:14 to the Gentiles in Christ Jesus, that we might
receive the promise of the Spirit through faith.
2 Tim. The Lord be with your spirit. Grace be with you.
4:22

"So then there remains a Sabbath rest for the people of
God....Let us therefore be diligent to enter into that rest lest
anyone fall after the same example of disobedience"(Heb. 4:9, 11).
What is this rest? We have to look at another type in the Old
Testament to discover its meaning. After the Israelites were
delivered and saved from the land of Egypt, they were brought
into the wilderness with the intention that they should go on into
the land of Canaan. The land of Canaan was their land of rest, a
type of the all-inclusive Christ. Christ is the good land of Canaan,
and He is our rest. If we are going to enter into the rest, we must
enter into Christ. But where is Christ today? We answer that He
is in our spirit. The Israelites, who were delivered out of Egypt,
instead of going on into Canaan, wandered for many years in the
wilderness. What does this typify? It means that many Christians
after being saved are simply wandering in the soul. The reason
the book to the Hebrews was written is that many Hebrew
Christians were saved, but they were wandering in their soul.
They would not press on from the wilderness into the good
land—that is, into Christ who dwelt in their spirit. We must not
continue to wander in our soul, but press on to enter into our
spirit, where Christ is our rest. (*The Economy of God,* pp. 30-31)

Today's Reading

Even though we may have been saved for years, we must
ask ourselves whether we are presently a Christian living in

the body, in the soul, or in the spirit. Are we now in Egypt, in the wilderness, or in the good land of Canaan? Ask the Lord and search yourself in order to be clear where you are. Frankly, many Christians are wandering all day in the soul, that is, in the wilderness. In the morning they have smiling faces, but by afternoon they are sorrowful with long faces. Yesterday, it seems they were in the heavens, but today they are down. They are wandering in the soul, the wilderness, without rest, circling in the same rut day after day. They may have been following the Lord for twenty years, but are still going in circles, just as the people of Israel, who wandered for thirty-eight years with no improvement and no progress. Why? Because they are in the soul. When we are in the soul, we are in the wilderness.

This is why the writer to the Hebrews emphasized the need to divide the soul from the spirit. The Word of God must pierce us so that we may know how to press on from the soul into the good land and the Holy of Holies of our human spirit. A soulish believer is one wandering in the wilderness of the soul, where there is no rest.

The High Priest had to pass through the veil in order to enter into the Holy of Holies; so the veil, which typifies the flesh (Heb. 10:20), must be riven and broken. Furthermore, the people of Israel had to cross the river of Jordan in order to enter the good land. Under the waters of the Jordan they buried twelve stones, representing the twelve tribes of Israel, and another twelve stones, representing the resurrected Israelites, were brought over into the good land. The old generation of Israel was buried in the death-waters of the Jordan River. All of this typifies that the natural man, the soulish life, or the old nature must be broken as the veil and buried as the old man. Then we can enter into the Holy of Holies and into the good land in order to enjoy Christ as our rest. (*The Economy of God,* pp. 32-33)

Further Reading: Life-study of Matthew, msg. 6; The Economy of God, ch. 3; The Issue of Christ Being Glorified by the Father with the Divine Glory, ch. 4

Enlightenment and inspiration: _____

_____

_____

> ### *Morning Nourishment*
>
> **Rom. 1:9** For God is my witness, whom I serve in my
> spirit in the gospel of His Son...
> **8:16** The Spirit Himself witnesses with our spirit
> that we are children of God.
> **1 Cor. 6:17** But he who is joined to the Lord is one spirit.
> **2 Cor. 2:13** I had no rest in my spirit, for I did not find Titus
> my brother...
> **13:14** The grace of the Lord Jesus Christ and the love
> of God and the fellowship of the Holy Spirit be
> with you all.
>
> The whole history of the children of Israel is a complete type
> of the experiences of the New Testament Christians (1 Cor.
> 10:6a, 11). Many Christians are clear that the Passover (1 Cor.
> 5:7), the exodus from Egypt (1 Cor. 10:1-2), the wandering in the
> wilderness (Heb. 3:7-19), and the enjoyment of the heavenly
> manna and the water out of the cleft rock (1 Cor. 10:3-4) are all
> types of our Christian experience today. But most Christians
> are not so clear that the entering into the good land and the
> living, walking, working, and laboring in the good land are also
> a type of our Christian experience (Col. 2:6-7). Our need is to
> know more and more about the living, the walking, the working,
> the laboring, and also the fighting of the people of Israel in the
> good land. (*An Autobiography of a Person in the Spirit*, p. 17)

Today's Reading

When Paul wrote these two letters, he must have had the
background of this history. In 1 Corinthians 5:7 he said that
Christ was our Passover. Then in chapter ten he told us that today
we are enjoying the heavenly manna and are drinking the living
water out of the cleft rock (vv. 3-4). This means that in 1 Corinthians the people had been brought out of Egypt and were
wandering in the wilderness. This was the real situation of the
Corinthians, and in this respect, many of today's Christians are
Corinthians....Some talk about the heavenly church in the book
of Ephesians, but not many are heavenly themselves. One can

talk about the good land, about Canaan, but he may still be in Egypt or in the wilderness. When you are in your spirit, you are in the heavenlies (Eph. 2:6) because the heavenlies cannot be separated from your spirit....Whenever you are living in the spirit, you are uplifted and you are in the heavenlies. But do you think that today you are walking completely in the spirit?

A spiritual man (1 Cor. 2:15) is one who does not behave according to the flesh nor act according to the soulish life, but lives according to the spirit, that is, his spirit (Rom. 1:9) mingled with the Spirit of God (Rom. 8:16; 1 Cor. 6:17). Such a one is dominated, governed, directed, moved, and led by such a mingled spirit. Although the Corinthians spoke much about spiritual things, the apostle Paul designated them as fleshly and soulish. They were talking about spiritual things in the soul and in the flesh. Some may talk about the heavenly things in Ephesians, but they do so as Corinthians—in the soul or in the flesh.

Paul's second Epistle to the Corinthians is much deeper than the first. It seems that not many have paid attention to this second book. In Romans there is justification by faith, and in Ephesians is the church as the Body of Christ. But what is the subject of 2 Corinthians? What is the impression that you get from this book? I must tell you that this book is absolutely in the spirit. Many Christians are living in their flesh or soul, not in their spirit. Many know something about the Holy Spirit, but too few know about their human spirit in which the Holy Spirit dwells....After the flesh and the soul in 1 Corinthians, we come to the spirit in 2 Corinthians. After the outer court and the Holy Place, we come to the Holy of Holies; after Egypt and the wilderness, we come to the good land, the land of Canaan. In this book you can see the good land. You can also see the practical life in the Holy of Holies. In this book you can see some human beings absolutely in the spirit. (*An Autobiography of a Person in the Spirit*, pp. 17-19)

Further Reading: An Autobiography of a Person in the Spirit, chs. 2, 10

Enlightenment and inspiration: Christ
being portion for us.

Morning Nourishment

1 Cor. But to us God has revealed *them* through the Spirit,
2:10-11 for the Spirit searches all things, even the depths
of God. For who among men knows the things of
man, except the spirit of man which is in him? In
the same way, the things of God also no one has
known except the Spirit of God.
Mark And immediately Jesus, knowing fully in His
2:8 spirit that they were reasoning this way within
themselves...

The way to experience all the aspects of Christ revealed in
1 Corinthians 1 and 2 is through the two spirits, the divine Spirit
and the regenerated human spirit. In 2:10 Paul speaks of the
divine Spirit, and in verse 11 he goes on to speak of the human
spirit....This verse indicates that if we would know the things
of man, we must use our human spirit, and if we would know
the things of God, we must do so by the Spirit of God.

When we exercise our spirit to know the things of man, we
are ushered into the Spirit of God. The two spirits, the regenerated human spirit and the divine Spirit, cannot be separated.
This is the reason Paul speaks of both spirits in 2:11. First he
says that no one knows the things of man except the spirit of
man which is in him. Then he goes on to say that the things of
God no one knows except the Spirit of God. If we would be a
proper and genuine human being, we must have these two
spirits. We must have the spirit of man to know the things of
man and the Spirit of God to know the things of God. According
to the Bible, the things of man are related to the things of God.
This makes it all the more necessary for us to have these two
spirits. (*Life-study of 1 Corinthians*, pp. 162-164)

Today's Reading

To be spiritual is to have your spirit, the regenerated human
spirit, mingled with the Spirit of God to become one spirit.
Spiritual persons live in this mingled spirit. Whenever you are

in the mingled spirit, you are spiritual, and you have spiritual discernment, spiritual knowledge, and spiritual communication. You are able to discern spiritually both the things of man and the things of God.

In 1 Corinthians 1 and 2 we see that Paul is an example of a person who knows the things of man and also the things of God....Although they did not know themselves, Paul knew [the Corinthians] very well, for he was a person who exercised his spirit in order to be ushered into the Spirit of God. By means of these two spirits, Paul had a thorough knowledge of the Corinthians.

Exercising our spirit ushers us into the Spirit of God. God's Spirit enables us to know not only where we are wrong, but also that God loves us and that Christ wants to be our life and our person. By the Spirit of God we may also know Christ as wisdom to us from God. Then if we continue to live in the mingled spirit, in our human spirit with the Spirit of God, we shall discover that Christ is our daily righteousness, sanctification, and redemption. We shall experience Him and enjoy Him. We shall also sense our need for the church and shall desire to come to the meetings, even though others may criticize us and wonder what we are doing.

If we use our spirit, we shall first come to know ourselves. In particular, we shall know where we are wrong in our position, condition, and situation. We shall also know where we are missing the mark of the divine provisions God has predestined, prepared, revealed, and given to us. Then we shall make confession to the Lord and seek His forgiveness. Eventually, we shall realize that the Spirit of God dwells in us and that He is eager to show us how much Christ loves us and how rich He is to us for our experience and enjoyment. This will cause us to enjoy the Lord and to have an increased desire for the church life. This is the experience of the spirit of man knowing the things of man and the Spirit of God knowing the things of God. (*Life-study of 1 Corinthians,* pp. 164, 175-176, 192-193)

Further Reading: Life-study of 1 Corinthians, msgs. 17-21

Enlightenment and inspiration: _____
_____
_____
_____

Morning Nourishment

1 Cor. **A man should account us in this way, as servants**
4:1 **of Christ and stewards of the mysteries of God.**
2:13 **Which things also we speak, not in words taught**
by human wisdom but in words taught by the
Spirit, interpreting spiritual things with spiri-
tual *words*.
16 **For who has known the mind of the Lord and will**
instruct Him? But we have the mind of Christ.

The subject of 1 Corinthians 4 is stewards of the mysteries of God (4:1-21). The focus of this chapter is neither Christ nor the church; it is the stewards of God's mysteries. In 4:1 Paul says, "A man should account us in this way, as servants of Christ and stewards of the mysteries of God." The Greek word rendered *stewards* in this verse is of the same root as the word *economy* or *dispensation* in 1 Timothy 1:4 and Ephesians 1:10. It means a dispensing steward, a household administrator, one who dispenses the household supply to its members. The apostles were appointed by the Lord to be such stewards, dispensing God's mysteries, which are Christ as the mystery of God and the church as the mystery of Christ (Col. 2:2; Eph. 3:4), to the believers. The dispensing service, the stewardship, is the ministry of the apostles. (*Life-study of 1 Corinthians*, p. 297)

Today's Reading

Paul says that he did not speak the spiritual things in words taught by human wisdom, but in words taught by the Spirit [1 Cor. 2:13]. This means that he did not speak in the words of Greek philosophy or wisdom. Rather, he communicated spiritual things by spiritual words. In this verse, Paul uses the same term with two meanings. First, *spiritual things* refers to the spiritual things themselves, the deep things of God concerning Christ. Second, the expression refers to spiritual words.... These spiritual words are spiritual things used to designate spiritual things.

The believers at Corinth talked about Christ not in spiritual words, but in the words of Greek philosophy and wisdom. As a result, they impressed others with philosophy, not with Christ. Paul, however, did not use philosophical terms when he spoke concerning Christ. Instead, he spoke spiritual things by spiritual words. He used spiritual words which are equal to the spiritual things themselves. In verse 13 Paul seems to be saying to the Corinthians, "I cannot use words of Greek wisdom to communicate spiritual things. These are words taught by man's wisdom. As such, they are not spiritual things, and they are of no avail in communicating spiritual things. If I used the wisdom of words admired by you Greeks, I would not be able to speak spiritual things to you."

We all should learn from Paul not to try to speak in the common expressions of the people. This means that we should not lower the standard of our preaching to the standard of common human expression. Ordinary human expression is not adequate to convey spiritual things. As soon as we depart from the standard of Spirit-taught language to the words taught by human wisdom, we shall no longer be able to convey spiritual things to others. For this reason, in my speaking and writing I endeavor to remain in the words taught by the Spirit.

Verse 16 is a conclusion to this portion of 1 Corinthians....Because we are organically one with Christ, we have all the faculties He has. The mind is the intelligence faculty, the understanding organ. We have such an organ of Christ so we can know what He knows. We have not only the life of Christ but also His mind. Christ must saturate our mind from our spirit, making our mind one with His. When we are one with Christ, His mind becomes our mind. This should not merely be a doctrine to us; it must be both our experience and our practice. (*Life-study of 1 Corinthians,* pp. 154-155, 157-158)

Further Reading: Life-study of 1 Corinthians, msgs. 17, 34

Enlightenment and inspiration: _____

_____

_____

_____

Hymns, #781

1   Exercise the spirit,
    Pray in every way!
    I have prayed too little,
    Keen my spirit, nay.
    Even when I prayed, my
    Spirit seldom proved
    Ever just to follow
    As Thy Spirit moved.

2   Now I'd pray in spirit
    As Thy Spirit groans;
    Pray by the anointing,
    Not as memory owns.
    Not the mind applying,
    But with spirit pray,
    Praising or beseeching,
    Spirit-led alway.

3   Not just by myself my
    Spirit exercise,
    But with others praying
    I would do likewise;
    Praying in the spirit,
    As the spirit wants,
    For 'tis in the inmost
    Spirits have response.

4   When we serve together,
    We thru prayer would move,
    Fellowship in spirit,
    Not in word to prove.
    Never pray together,
    Shouting, crying much,
    Yet the fellowship in
    Spirit never touch.

5   Exercise the spirit
    Here and everywhere,
    Few or many present,
    Caring not who's there.
    Not a place or person
    Will influence me,
    In all kinds of meetings
    I'll my spirit free.

6 Thus my spirit lifted
Gives the Lord His way;
Thus, my spirit strengthened,
I'll be used each day.
In the spirit's flowing
Living water see;
Thus the saints are mingled,
Built the church will be.

Composition for prophecy with main point and sub-points: _____

_____

_____

_____

_____

_____

_____

_____

_____

_____

_____

_____

_____

_____

_____

_____

_____

_____

_____

_____

_____

_____

_____

_____

_____

_____

_____

_____

_____

_____

_____

Growing Christ as the Precious Materials for God's Building

Scripture Reading: 1 Cor. 3:1-17

Day 1 I. **God's goal is to have a farm that will grow materials for the building up of His holy temple as His dwelling place (3:6-7, 9, 12, 16-17).**

II. **The believers, who have been regenerated in Christ with God's life, are God's cultivated land, a farm in God's new creation to grow Christ that precious materials may be produced for God's building (cf. 4:15).**

III. **Paul regarded all the believers in Christ as plants which need growth (3:6-7):**

A. In verse 1 Paul refers to the believers at Corinth as infants in Christ; their need was to grow in life to maturity, to be full-grown (2:6; Col. 1:28).

B. The reason for division and lack of building is that the believers remain in their natural life and natural being (1 Cor. 1:12-13; 3:3-4; 2:14).

Day 2 C. The Corinthians, who were still infants with respect to the initial gifts, desperately needed to grow (3:2; 1:7):

1. The Corinthians exhibited three signs of infancy:

a. Being unable to receive solid food but only milk (3:2).

b. Being full of jealousy and strife and walking according to man (1:11; 3:3).

c. Exalting spiritual giants to cause divisions (1:12; 3:4).

2. The initial gifts—the divine life and the Holy Spirit (Rom. 6:23; Acts 2:38; Heb. 6:4)—are the seed sown into us (Mark 4:26); now these gifts need to be developed and cultivated:

a. In 1 Corinthians Paul is seeking to develop

and cultivate the initial gifts received by the believers.

    b. What we need in the Lord's recovery, and what the Lord is seeking among us, is more growth in life, more development of the initial gifts.

  D. The life with which the believers grow in the church is the crucified and resurrected Christ (1 Cor. 2:2; Col. 3:4).

  E. The growth in life is caused by God; as far as the growth in life is concerned, all the ministers of Christ are nothing, and God is everything (1 Cor. 3:6-7).

  F. God's desire is that our heart would be open to Him, soft toward Him, and longing for Him, and that we would draw near to Him, eat Him, drink Him, enjoy Him, and digest Him that daily we would grow with the growth of God (10:3-4; Col. 2:19).

Day 3   IV. **The Lord Jesus came as a Sower to sow God into us; we are the earth, the cultivated land, the farm, to grow Christ (Mark 4:3-4, 14; 1 Cor. 3:9):**

  A. God's farm grows Christ, and Christ is for the building (v. 11); as Christians, we are growing Christ.

  B. When we grow properly, Christ will be produced in us; the issue of our growth will be Christ (Eph. 4:15; Col. 2:19; Gal. 4:19).

  C. The church is built with the Christ we experience and who is even the produce grown by us (1 Cor. 3:12):

    1. For the building up of the church, we must have the Christ who is produced through our growth in life.

    2. There can be no building without the growing of Christ as the material for God's building; as God's farm, we must grow in life to produce Christ.

Day 4

V. **The church is God's farm which produces gold, silver, and precious stones (vv. 9, 12):**

A. The church, the temple of God, must be built with gold, silver, and precious stones produced from Christ's growing in us (vv. 16-17).

B. First we have the growth on God's farm; then the plants on this farm become the precious materials for God's building (vv. 6-7, 12).

C. Gold, silver, and precious stones signify the various experiences of Christ in the virtues and attributes of the Triune God; these precious materials are the products of our enjoyment of Christ (v. 12; 15:45b; 6:17).

D. The precious materials for God's building are related to the Triune God—to the Father's nature, the Son's redemption, and the Spirit's transforming work (2 Pet. 1:4; Eph. 1:7; Heb. 9:12; 2 Cor. 3:18).

Day 5

E. We are becoming gold, silver, and precious stones for God's building (1 Cor. 3:12):

1. In God the Father, we have His life and nature as the gold; in God the Son, we have His redemption as the silver; and in God the Spirit, we have transformation as the precious stones.

2. In order to build with these materials, we ourselves must be constituted with them; we need to be constituted with the Father's nature, the Son's redemption, and the Spirit's transformation.

3. We need the growth in the nature of God the Father, the redemption of God the Son, and the transformation of God the Spirit; this growth makes us gold, silver, and precious stones for God's building (vv. 12, 16-17).

4. Through digestion, assimilation, and metabolism, Christ becomes us, and we become Him; then we become the precious materials for God's building (Eph. 3:17; Gal. 4:19).

Day 6   **VI. God's eternal goal is the building—the temple built with precious materials on Christ as the unique foundation (1 Cor. 3:11-12, 16-17):**

A. The growth in the divine life produces precious materials for the building of God's habitation; this habitation, the church, is the increase, the enlargement, of the unlimited Christ (Eph. 2:21-22; John 3:29-34).

B. First we have the farm for the growth in life; then we have the building for God's eternal purpose (1 Cor. 3:9; Matt. 16:18; Eph. 2:20-22; 4:16).

C. The actual building of the church as the house of God is by the growth in life of the believers (1 Cor. 3:6-7, 16-17; Eph. 2:20-21; 1 Pet. 2:2-5):

1. True building is the growth in life; the extent to which we have been built up is the extent to which we have grown.

2. In order to have the genuine building, we need to grow by having ourselves reduced and by having Christ increased within us (Matt. 16:24; Eph. 3:17).

Morning Nourishment

1 Cor. I gave you milk to drink, not solid food, for you
  3:2   were not yet able *to receive it.* But neither yet
        now are you able.
   6   I planted, Apollos watered, but God caused the
        growth.
Col.   And not holding the Head, out from whom all the
2:19   Body, being richly supplied and knit together by
        means of the joints and sinews, grows with the
        growth of God.

We have to see...that the real building of the house of God depends on our growth in life. The more we grow, the more we are built up. Our growth in life is the increase of God in us. God's desire is that our heart would be open to Him, soft toward Him, and longing for Him, and that we would draw near to Him, eat Him, drink Him, enjoy Him, and digest Him inwardly, so that daily we would grow with the increase of God. Furthermore, God's desire is that in all things we would learn to grow up into Christ, the Head, to submit under His authority, and to be under His ruling. If we would be serious about learning the lessons in all these matters, then God would be able to do the building work in us daily. (*The Building Work of God*, p. 40)

Today's Reading

Although the saints may water others, growth comes only from God Himself [1 Cor. 3:6-7]....Because growth comes from God alone, those who water others must help them contact God. Actually, contacting God is itself the watering. Thus, the best way to be watered is to contact God. If you can help a weaker one or a young one have some contact with God, that will bring in the genuine watering. The watering will then supply the ingredients of life to those who already possess the divine life. As these ingredients are added to them, they will have an additional supply of life. Then spontaneously they will grow.

[First Corinthians] reveals that Christ is the unique center of God's economy and also our portion for our enjoyment. This wonderful One is now the life-giving Spirit dwelling in our spirit. Continually we need to exercise our spirit to be one spirit with Him. The more we contact the Lord in this way, the more we are watered, supplied, and nourished. Then spontaneously we shall grow. I thank the Lord that many of the saints in the churches throughout the world are experiencing the genuine growth in life. What we need in the Lord's recovery, and what the Lord is seeking among us, is more growth in life, more development of the initial gifts.

We have seen that in 3:1 Paul indicates that the believers at Corinth were infants in Christ. They, of course, had been genuinely saved, but they were fleshly and even fleshy, not spiritual. They exhibited the signs of infancy: not able to receive solid food, but only milk; being full of jealousy and strife and walking according to man; and exalting spiritual giants to cause divisions.

Paul knew that the Corinthian believers needed feeding, watering, and the additional supply of life. They needed to be fed with solid food (v. 2), they needed to be watered continually (vv. 6-7), and they needed the additional supply of life from God so that they could grow in life. These are the very things we need in the church life today. We need to be fed with solid food. We also need to water others and to be watered ourselves. We have seen that even the youngest and weakest among us is able to water the saints. But in watering others we should not try to solve their problems or presume to do God's work by trying to help others grow. Instead, we should simply take time to contact God together. Then others will be watered, and God will give them growth through the additional life supply. May we all see that what is urgently needed is the growth in life. May we live in a way which produces the growth in life, and may we function by planting, feeding, watering, and also by leaving the actual growth to God. (*Life-study of 1 Corinthians*, pp. 216-217)

Further Reading: The Building Work of God, ch. 3; Life-study of 1 Corinthians, msgs. 23-25; The Conclusion of the New Testament, msg. 108

Enlightenment and inspiration: _____
_____
_____
_____

Morning Nourishment

1 Cor. So that you do not lack in any gift, eagerly await-
1:7 ing the revelation of our Lord Jesus Christ.

3:7 So then neither is he who plants anything nor he
who waters, but God who causes the growth.

Rom. For the wages of sin is death, but the gift of God
6:23 is eternal life in Christ Jesus our Lord.

Acts And Peter said to them, Repent and each one of
2:38 you be baptized upon the name of Jesus Christ
for the forgiveness of your sins, and you will
receive the gift of the Holy Spirit.

In 1 Corinthians 1:7 *gift* refers to the inward gifts issuing from grace, such as the free gift of eternal life (Rom. 6:23) and the gift of the Holy Spirit (Acts 2:38) as the heavenly gift (Heb. 6:4), not the outward, miraculous gifts, such as healing or speaking in tongues, in chapters twelve and fourteen. All the inward gifts are parts of grace. They are the initial things of the divine life received of grace. All these need to grow (1 Cor. 3:6-7) to their full development and maturity. The Corinthian believers were not lacking in the initial gifts in life, but they were desperately short of the growth in life. Hence, however much they were initially enriched in grace, they were still infants in Christ, soulish, fleshly, and even fleshy (2:14; 3:1, 3). (*Life-study of 1 Corinthians*, p. 18)

Today's Reading

After many years, I now have the boldness to say that the gift in 1:7 is different from the gifts spoken of in chapters twelve and fourteen. In these two chapters some gifts are miraculous and others are mature....As we have pointed out, the gift in verse 7 refers to the initial gifts issuing from grace, namely eternal life and the gift of the Holy Spirit. At the time of our regeneration, we received eternal life as the gift of God. According to Acts 2:38, the Holy Spirit also is a gift. To speak of these gifts as initial gifts indicates that these gifts have not yet developed; they have not yet grown to maturity.

The growth of a plant from a seed to a mature plant illustrates the growth and development of the initial gifts. First, a seed is sown into the ground. This seed is the initial plant. As the seed grows, it develops until it reaches maturity. The Corinthian believers all had the initial gifts; they all had the divine life and the Holy Spirit sown into them as seeds....Here Paul was telling the Corinthians this: "You believers in Corinth have received the Lord Jesus. When you believed in Him, you received the initial gifts—the divine life and the Holy Spirit. The problem is that you have not allowed these gifts to grow and develop." For this reason, in chapter three Paul points out that the Corinthians need to grow. He says, "I planted, Apollos watered, but God caused the growth" (1 Cor. 3:6). The Corinthians, still infants with respect to the initial gifts, desperately needed to grow.

An infant has life and also the functions of life, but no growth or development of life. This makes it impossible for him to do anything. The more a child grows, the more he is able to do. For example, my eleven-year-old grandson can do many things which his younger brother, aged seven, is not able to do. Even four years' growth makes a great difference. This does not mean that the younger boy does not have life. He has life, but does not have the same amount of the development of this life. Likewise, even though the Corinthians had received the initial gifts and had been enriched in Christ in all expression and in all knowledge, they were still infants. The initial gifts had not been developed.

The Epistle of 1 Corinthians was written to philosophical people. We should not think, however, that the ancient Greeks were more philosophical than we are today. We all are philosophical. Like the Corinthians, we philosophical ones have been enriched in our understanding concerning spiritual things. We may have the knowledge of these things, yet still be babes in Christ. (*Life-study of 1 Corinthians*, pp. 18-19)

Further Reading: Life-study of 1 Corinthians, msg. 2; The Experience of Christ as Life for the Building Up of the Church, ch. 4

Enlightenment and inspiration: _____

_____

_____

Morning Nourishment

1 Cor. I planted, Apollos watered, but God caused the
3:6 growth.
9 For we are God's fellow workers; you are God's
cultivated land, God's building.
Eph. But holding to truth in love, we may grow up into
4:15 Him in all things, who is the Head, Christ.
Gal. My children, with whom I travail again in birth
4:19 until Christ is formed in you.

Planted, watered, and *caused the growth* (1 Cor. 3:6) are all
related to the matter of life. This indicates that the believers are
God's farm to grow Christ. As plants on God's farm, the church,
we need to grow. Without growth, we are useless....There are
many believers today who are alive spiritually, but they do not
grow. Of course, it is better to live than to die. As long as we are
alive, we have the opportunity to grow. I hope that no one in the
Lord's recovery will be content to live without growing. We all
must grow to produce Christ. All the saints in the Lord's
recovery must be desperate to grow. We should pray, "Lord,
grant me the growth." (*Life-study of 1 Corinthians,* p. 198)

Today's Reading

The central point of these messages on 1 Corinthians 3 is
growing to produce Christ. As a help in growing Christ, we need
to consider chapters one and two again and again. If you read
and pray-read these chapters, you will be watered and nourished. The very element and substance of Christ will be imparted into your being. Then spontaneously you will grow and
produce Christ. The issue of your growth will be Christ.

Paul's intention in 1 Corinthians 1 and 2 is to present Christ
as our portion, enjoyment, life, living, content, and everything.
Christ should be our one choice, preference, taste, and enjoyment. We should enjoy Christ to such an extent that we do not
care for culture of any kind. Instead of living culture, we live
Christ. Christ becomes everything to us in our daily living—our
culture, our ethics, and our morality.

When we grow properly, Christ will be produced in us. Then whatever we grow of Christ will become the materials for God's building. The church is built only with Christ. However, the church is not built with the objective Christ, with a Christ who is in the heavens or who suddenly descends from the heavens. On the contrary, the church is built with the Christ we experience and who is even the produce grown by us. Thus, for the building of the church, we must have the Christ who is produced through our growth in life.

The materials used for the building of the tabernacle were called heave offerings. This means that the materials created by God had to be gained, possessed, enjoyed, and treasured by God's redeemed people. Then the people were to bring these materials and present them to God as heave offerings. Only materials gained, possessed, and offered in this way could be the proper materials for the building of the tabernacle. This signifies that we need to gain, possess, and enjoy the riches of Christ until they become our treasure. Then we need to bring what we have experienced of Christ to the church meetings and offer this Christ to the Lord as a heave offering. This Christ will then become the materials used for the building up of the church.

Building the church is not merely a matter of preaching the gospel, saving sinners, and bringing these newly saved ones into a so-called church. This is not the building up of the church; it is the piling up of raw materials....Now that we have seen that we are God's farm, we must grow in the divine life to produce Christ.

In 1:6 Paul says, "I planted, Apollos watered, but God caused the growth." If we would grow Christ on God's farm, we need the planting and the watering. However, we should not think that only those such as Paul and Apollos are responsible for planting and watering. All the brothers and sisters in the church should carry out this work. (*Life-study of 1 Corinthians,* pp. 198-200)

Further Reading: Life-study of 1 Corinthians, msg. 22; *The Divine Dispensing of the Divine Trinity,* ch. 29

Enlightenment and inspiration: _____
_____
_____
_____

Morning Nourishment

1 Cor. 3:9 ...You are God's cultivated land, God's building.
12 But if anyone builds upon the foundation gold, silver, precious stones, wood, grass, stubble.
2 Pet. 1:4 ...That through these you might become partakers of the divine nature...
2 Cor. 3:18 But we all with unveiled face, beholding and reflecting like a mirror the glory of the Lord, are being transformed into the same image from glory to glory, even as from the Lord Spirit.

In 1 Corinthians 3 Paul seems to be saying, "You Corinthian believers should no longer seek to be wise. Instead, you should be plants growing on God's farm. There is no need for you to philosophize so much. You should be simple and know nothing except Christ. Then you will grow in Him and with Him, and you will even grow Him. Eventually, in your growth, you will be transformed and become the gold, silver, and precious stones as the materials for the building up of God's temple...."

Wood refers to our nature, our natural makeup, grass to our being, and stubble to our doings. We should never use our nature, our being, or our doings to build the church. Instead, we must renounce all these things and reject them. For the proper building we need to enjoy, experience, and possess the nature of God the Father and the redemptive work of the Son. As we experience the Father and the Son in this way, we shall be in our spirit with the Spirit of God. Spontaneously the outcome, the issue, will be precious stones. If we build with gold, silver, and precious stones, we shall build with the proper materials on Christ as the only foundation. (*Life-study of 1 Corinthians*, pp. 251-252)

Today's Reading

Gold, silver, and precious stones [1 Cor. 3:12] signify various experiences of Christ in the virtues and attributes of the Triune God. It is with these the apostles and all spiritual believers build the church on the unique foundation of Christ. Gold may signify the divine nature of the Father with all its attributes, silver may signify the redeeming Christ with all the virtues and attributes of His Person and work, and precious stones may signify the transforming work of the Spirit with all its attributes. All these precious materials are the products of our participation in and enjoyment of Christ in our spirit through the Holy Spirit. Only these are good for God's building.

As God's farm with planting, watering, and growing, the church should produce plants. But the proper materials for the building up of the church are gold, silver, and precious stones, all of which are minerals. Hence, the thought of transformation is implied here. We need not only to grow in life, but also to be transformed in life, as revealed in 2 Corinthians 3:18 and Romans 12:2. This corresponds to the thought in the Lord's parables in Matthew 13 concerning wheat, mustard seed, and meal (all of which are botanical) and the treasure hidden in the earth, gold and precious stones (minerals).

The church is a farm which produces gold, silver, and precious stones. These are minerals and are usually mined from the earth. But in chapter three we have a farm that eventually produces gold, silver, and precious stones. This implies that as the plants on God's farm grow, they eventually become minerals. The plants, of course, are botanical in nature. But as they grow, they are transformed into minerals. Thus, in this chapter, we have both growth in life and transformation. Whatever is grown on God's farm is eventually transformed in nature. Transformation does not involve mere outward change, but an inward, organic, metabolic change. In the New Testament transformation involves metabolism, a process in which a new element is added into our being to replace the old element. Hence, transformation is a metabolic change.... Growth produces transformation and even becomes transformation. The more we grow as plants, the more we become minerals. (*Life-study of 1 Corinthians,* pp. 233-234)

Further Reading: Life-study of 1 Corinthians, msgs. 26-28; *The Divine Dispensing of the Divine Trinity,* ch. 29

Enlightenment and inspiration: _____

_____

_____

_____

Morning Nourishment

1 Cor. But if anyone builds upon the foundation gold,
3:12 silver, precious stones, wood, grass, stubble.
  16 Do you not know that you are the temple of God,
     and *that* the Spirit of God dwells in you?
Eph. That Christ may make His home in your hearts
3:17 through faith, that you, being rooted and
     grounded in love.

We have seen that gold, silver, and precious stones refer to
God the Father, God the Son, and God the Spirit. Now we must
go on to see what it means to build with these materials. In
order to build with these materials, we ourselves must first be
constituted of them. We need to be constituted of the Father's
nature, the Son's redemption, and the Spirit's transformation.
This means that we must be constituted of the Triune God.
When we receive Him, when we take Him into us by drinking
Him and eating Him, when we are transfused with Him and by
Him, the very Triune God—the Father, the Son, and the Spirit—
comes into us to be our element and substance. This causes a
metabolic process to take place within us by which a new
element is added and an old element is discharged. Another
name for this process is transformation.

Transformation does not take place overnight. On the contrary, it is a work which goes on continually day by day. As we
call on the Lord Jesus, praise the Father, read and pray-read
the Word, pray, sing, worship, attend the meetings of the church,
and fellowship with the saints, we take the Triune God into us.
The more we receive of Him, the more His element transforms
us metabolically and causes us to be constituted of Himself.
Then we have gold, silver, and precious stones. (*Life-study of
1 Corinthians,* pp. 280-281)

Today's Reading

In order for the food we eat to become our constitution, there
must be the process of metabolism. In the Bible this process is called
transformation. Transformation involves a metabolic change.

Hence, transformation is altogether a metabolic process. First we eat a meal. After a period of time, the food is digested and assimilated. Eventually, the digested and assimilated food becomes the fibers of our being. This is metabolism, transformation. In order for an infant of seven pounds to grow into a mature man weighing one hundred seventy pounds, there must be a regular eating and a normal process of metabolism. Gradually, the food taken in by an infant will cause him to grow. Eventually, as a result of a metabolic process over a long period of time, he will become a full-grown man. As a mature man, he is a product, a composition, of all the food he has eaten, digested, and assimilated. This illustrates the process of spiritual metabolism. The produce grown on the farm is eaten and digested by us. Eventually, through the process of metabolism, this food supply becomes us and transforms us into material for the building up of the Body of Christ.

The church is a farm to grow Christ. Every item of the produce grown on the farm is Christ. The farm produce includes many different aspects of Christ. Christ is the milk, the vegetables, and the meat. The church grows Christ, and all the saints eat Christ. Eventually, through digestion, assimilation, and metabolism, Christ becomes us, and we become Him. Then we are the proper materials for the building.

Paul's writing in 1 Corinthians 3 has a direct connection from item to item. First he refers to feeding, drinking, and eating. Then he goes on to mention planting and watering, after which he tells us that it is God alone who gives the growth. Following this, he says in verse 9 that we are the farm and the building. Therefore, there is a direct connection between all these matters. As we have seen, the farm becomes the building. (*Life-study of 1 Corinthians,* pp. 272-273)

Further Reading: Life-study of 1 Corinthians, msgs. 31-32; *The Economy and Dispensing of God,* ch. 7; *A Deeper Study of the Divine Dispensing,* ch. 10*

Enlightenment and inspiration: _____

_____

_____

_____

Morning Nourishment

1 Cor. 3:16 Do you not know that you are the temple of God, and *that* the Spirit of God dwells in you?

9 ...You are God's cultivated land, God's building.

Eph. 2:21 In whom all the building, being fitted together, is growing into a holy temple in the Lord.

4:16 Out from whom all the Body, being joined together and being knit together through every joint of the rich supply and *through* the operation in the measure of each one part, causes the growth of the Body unto the building up of itself in love.

God's purpose in coming into us in the form of food to be mingled with us as our life and to grow in us is to build a temple, which is the house of God. Therefore, in the Scriptures we often see that growth and building are linked together.

Nearly all of the verses listed at the beginning of 1 Corinthians 3 refer to both growth and building. First Corinthians 3:9b says, "You are God's cultivated land, God's building." As God's cultivated land, we need to grow; as God's building, we need to be built up. Therefore, growth is building, and building is growth; these two things cannot be separated. Hence, Ephesians 2 says that this spiritual house, this dwelling place of God, is built up by growing (vv. 21-22), just as our body reaches its full stature by growing. Moreover, 1 Peter 2 says that having been saved and having put away sins, we need to long for the spiritual milk so that we may grow (vv. 1-2). Following this, it says that as living stones we are being built up as a spiritual house (v. 5). Ephesians 4:12-13 says, "Unto the building up of the Body of Christ, until we all arrive...at a full-grown man." Without growth, there is no building up. The more we grow, the more we are built up. When we are fully grown, then the building will be complete. Hence, God's growth and mingling in us are God's building. (*The Building Work of God*, pp. 35-36)

Today's Reading

With a spiritual building, a building in life, the true building is the growth in life. The extent to which we have been built is the extent to which we have grown. To be built into the spiritual building does not first mean to be connected with others. It means to have our natural life reduced and to have Christ increased within us. The more our natural life is reduced and the more Christ increases within us, the easier it will be for us to coordinate with others. In fact, we shall be able to coordinate with anyone. However, some saints have told me that they cannot move from their locality because they have been built with certain saints in the church there. According to their concept, because they have been built together with these ones, it is not possible for them to leave that locality. This is not real building. On the contrary, it is friendship or some kind of social relationship. If you have truly been built into the church, you have been reduced, and Christ has been increased in you. Then, wherever you may be, you can be one with the saints and coordinate with them. Once you have been built into God's spiritual building, you can never be taken out of it.

As we have seen, the true building is to become reduced in our natural life and to have Christ increased within us. If this is our situation, we shall not have any preferences. If the Lord leads us to a place which is rather difficult, we shall praise Him for those hardships, knowing that they will cause us to be reduced even more and will create more room in our being for Christ. Then we shall have real growth, and we shall be happy with the church life.

We need the genuine building....The real building is to have ourselves reduced and to have Christ increased until we arrive at the measure of the stature of the fullness of Christ. (*Life-study of 1 Corinthians,* pp. 264-265, 267, 269)

Further Reading: The Experience of Christ as Life for the Building Up of the Church, chs. 4-5; Life-study of 1 Corinthians, msgs. 22, 25, 30; The Conclusion of the New Testament, msg. 208

Enlightenment and inspiration: _____

_____

_____

_____

Hymns, #1242

1   The Lord, the seed of life, has sown Himself into our heart
    To grow up into fullness and become His counterpart.
    The seed requires no rules or forms, for water is its need—
    By this the all-inclusive seed will grow in us indeed!
     The seed is simply Jesus! Oh, Jesus lives in me!
     And by His growth this seed in us will reach maturity.

2   The growth of Christ, the seed, in us will soon produce the wheat,
    The life within break forth—yet work divine is not complete;
    For wheat alone can never be the seed's expression true;
    So all the grains must blend together into something new.
     The seed is simply Jesus; now wheat is Jesus too!
     The grains of wheat must blend together into something new.

3   The individual grains of wheat no longer must be free,
    But crushed together, ground to powder, every grain must be,
    Until the wheat becomes the meal from which the loaf is formed
    Till all the saints will blend and to His Body be conformed.
     We all must take the grinding until the Christ within
     Can mold into His Body all the individual grains.

4   The seed is planted, wheat is grown and meal is the sum
    Of all the growth upon God's farm, where Christians grow as one;
    But all the growth in life is for the building of the church,
    That God and man may have a home and both may end their search.
     The farm is for the building, for God and man a home,
     Where both may dwell among His people gathered into one.

5   God's building is produced by silver, precious stones, and gold—
    From meal through transformation, pressure, heat, and pain untold.
    The meal must not be satisfied to stay as meal alone,
    But must submit to transformation into precious stone.
     The meal must pass through suffering that precious stones be formed;
     Then built into God's building, to His purpose full conformed.

6   From fullest growth and transformation comes a pearl of worth;
    This simple, precious, all-inclusive gem will then come forth.
    Conceived in death and formed in life by that all-glorious One,
    The church, His Bride, the fruit of all the work that He has done.
     The pearl is what He's after, the Bride to please His heart,
     So single, pure and precious, and His very counterpart.

7   The growth in life begins when planted on God's farm we're found;
    The growing seed becomes the wheat from which the meal is ground.
    But building work proceeds when meal submits to be transformed;
    Then gold and silver, precious stones for building will be formed.
    The farm is for the building, built up by precious stones,
    From which the priceless pearl comes forth to be His Bride, His own.

8   Lord, keep us poor in spirit, pure in heart that we may be
    Good ground in which the seed of life may grow abundantly,
    Until the final stage is reached and You are satisfied
    And have Your priceless, chosen pearl, Your joy complete, Your Bride.
    Lord, keep us poor in spirit and purified in heart,
    That growing up in us You may bring forth Your counterpart.

Composition for prophecy with main point and sub-points: _____

_____

_____

_____

_____

_____

_____

_____

_____

_____

_____

_____

_____

_____

_____

_____

_____

_____

_____

_____

_____

_____

_____

Being One Spirit with the Lord
to Have the Highest Spirituality

Scripture Reading: 1 Cor. 6:17-20; 7:17-25, 40

Day 1

I. **The essence of the New Testament is the two spirits—the divine Spirit and the human spirit—mingled together as one spirit (6:17; Rom. 8:4):**

A. The word *joined* in 1 Corinthians 6:17 refers to the believers' organic union with the Lord through believing into Him (John 3:15-16; 15:4-5).

B. The expression *one spirit* indicates the mingling of the Lord as the Spirit with our spirit:

1. The spirit, which is the mingling of our spirit and the Lord's Spirit into one spirit, is both the Spirit of the Lord and our spirit (Rom. 8:4; 2 Cor. 3:17; 1 Cor. 15:45b; 6:17).

2. All of our spiritual experiences, such as our fellowship with the Lord, our prayer to Him, and our living with Him, are in this mingled spirit.

C. The union of God and man is a union of the two spirits, the Spirit of God and the spirit of man (2:11-14); the union of these two spirits is the deepest mystery in the Bible.

D. The focus of God's economy is the mingled spirit, the divine Spirit mingled with the human spirit; whatever God intends to do or accomplish is related to this focus (Eph. 3:9, 5; 1:17; 2:22; 4:23; 5:18; 6:18).

Day 2

E. By being one spirit with the Lord, we can experience Him as the all-inclusive One (1 Cor. 1:2, 24, 30; 2:8, 10; 3:11; 5:7-8; 10:3-4; 11:3; 12:12; 15:20, 47, 45):

1. We enjoy Christ by being joined to Him as one spirit.

2. We can experience Christ and take Christ as everything because we have become one spirit with Him.

3. When we are one spirit with the Lord, we enjoy the fellowship of God's Son, Jesus Christ our Lord (1:9).
4. For everyone who is one spirit with the Lord, the supply is inexhaustible.

F. The spirit of faith (2 Cor. 4:13) is the Holy Spirit mingled with our human spirit; we should exercise such a spirit to believe and to speak the things that we have experienced of the Lord.

G. The Holy Spirit is in our spirit (Rom. 8:16), and our spirit is within our body; hence, our body becomes a temple of the Holy Spirit (1 Cor. 6:19-20):
1. Our organic union with the Lord makes it possible for our bodies to be members of Christ (v. 15).
2. Because we are organically united with Christ and because Christ dwells in our spirit (2 Tim. 4:22) and makes His home in our heart (Eph. 3:17), our entire being, including our purified body, becomes a member of Christ.
3. We urgently need to see the vision that our bodies are members of Christ, that we are one spirit with the Lord, and that our body is a temple of the Holy Spirit (1 Cor. 6:15, 17, 19).

Day 3

H. The mingled spirit is a spirit that is one spirit with God and that is the same as God in His life and nature but not in His Godhead (1 John 5:11; 2 Pet. 1:4):
1. The divine Spirit and the human spirit are mingled as one within us so that we can live the life of a God-man, a life that is God yet man and man yet God (Gal. 2:20; Phil. 1:19-21a).
2. The God-man living is the living of the two spirits, the Spirit of God and the spirit of man joined and mingled together as one.

Day 4 II. **First Corinthians 7 conveys the spirit of a person who loves the Lord, who cares for the Lord's interests on earth, who is absolutely for the Lord and one with the Lord, and who in every respect is obedient, submissive, and satisfied with God and the circumstances arranged by Him:**

A. Paul was absolutely one with God, and he wanted the Corinthian believers to be one with Him and not to initiate anything (vv. 17-24).

B. Because Paul was utterly one with the Lord, in his instructions and answers he spontaneously and unconsciously expressed an absolute spirit:

1. Paul had an excellent spirit, a spirit that was submissive, content, and satisfied:

   a. In his spirit he was very submissive and content with his situation.

   b. To him, every situation was of the Lord, and he would not initiate anything to change it.

2. Because Paul had such a spirit, he could answer the Corinthians in a way that would help them also to become one with God in their situation (v. 24).

Day 5 III. **Because Paul was one with the Lord, when he spoke, the Lord spoke with him; thus, in 1 Corinthians 7 we have an example of the New Testament principle of incarnation (vv. 10, 12, 25, 40):**

A. The principle of incarnation is that God enters into man and mingles Himself with man to make man one with Himself; thus, God is in man and man is in God (John 15:4-5):

1. In the New Testament the Lord becomes one with His apostles, and they become one with Him and speak together with Him; thus, His word becomes their word, and whatever they utter is His word.

2. The Old Testament principle of speaking for God was "Thus saith the Lord" (Isa. 10:24; Jer. 2:2); the New Testament principle of incarnation is "I [the speaker] charge," for the speaker and the Lord are one.

Day 6 B. Paul wrote 1 Corinthians 7 in the principle of incarnation:

1. The principle in verse 10 is the same as that in Galatians 2:20: the principle of incarnation—two persons living as one person.

2. Because Paul was one with the Lord, he knew the Lord's heart and mind.

3. Paul was one with the Lord to such a degree that when he gave his own opinion, he thought that he also had the Spirit of God (1 Cor. 7:40).

4. In verses 25 and 40 we see the highest spirituality—the spirituality of a person who is so one with the Lord and permeated with Him that even his opinion expresses the Lord's mind.

5. If we are saturated with the Spirit, what we express will be our thought, but it will also be something of the Lord because we are one with Him (6:17).

Morning Nourishment

1 Cor. 6:17 But he who is joined to the Lord is one spirit.
19 ...Your body is a temple of the Holy Spirit within you...
John 3:6 ...That which is born of the Spirit is spirit.
15 That every one who believes into Him may have eternal life.
Rom. 8:4 That the righteous requirement of the law might be fulfilled in us, who...walk...according to the spirit.
6 ...The mind set on the spirit is life and peace.

The word *joined* in 1 Corinthians 6:17 refers to the believers' organic union with the Lord through believing into Him (John 3:15-16). This union is illustrated by that of the branches with the vine (John 15:4-5). It is a matter not only of life, but also in life, the divine life. Such a union with the resurrected Lord can only be in our spirit.

The expression *one spirit* indicates the mingling of the Lord as the Spirit with our spirit. Our spirit has been regenerated by the Spirit of God (John 3:6), who is now in us (1 Cor. 6:19) and is one with our spirit (Rom. 8:16). This is the realization of the Lord who became the life-giving Spirit through resurrection (1 Cor. 15:45; 2 Cor. 3:17), and who is now with our spirit (2 Tim. 4:22). This mingled spirit is often referred to in Paul's Epistles, as in Romans 8:4-6.

We the believers are joined to the Lord as one spirit....Often I pray in the morning, "Lord, thank You for another day in which to practice being one spirit with You." What a wonder that sinners such as we can be one spirit with the Lord!...We need to experiment and learn how to be one spirit with the Lord in our speaking and in all that we do. As we do various things, we need to consider whether or not we are one spirit with the Lord. (*Life-study of 1 Corinthians,* pp. 345-346, 349-350)

Today's Reading

This matter of the mingled spirit is not just some vain

teaching. It is a fact which is too great! The fact is that the Spirit of God is not only living and true, but He is within you. Not only is He within you, but He is also mingling Himself with your spirit to make your spirit and Him one spirit (1 Cor. 6:17). If you could realize this in a thorough way, you would be excited. It is not a small thing! This is a very complicated matter. It is not a complication with two small things involved. It is a universal and great complication with God's Spirit and our spirit involved. Today these two spirits are just one (1 Cor. 6:17).

Although, according to your knowledge, you may be bold to tell me that your spirit is mingled with God's Spirit, I am concerned to look at your living. How do you live? Do you live a life by your spirit mingled with God's Spirit, or do you live a life by something else? I am afraid that this fact of the mingled spirit is in your understanding, but not in your living. The fact of the mingled spirit, our spirit mingled with God's Spirit, must not be merely our theology. This must be our reality in a living way.

When I talk to my wife I want to have the assurance that I am talking to her by my spirit mingled with the Spirit of God.... Today He is not only the living and true God, but He is mingled with our inner being. He is the Spirit mingled with our innermost being, and this innermost part of our being is our spirit.... It is a fact not only revealed in the living Word but also realized by our experience. In our experience I cannot deny such a fact. Without such a fact my living would be altogether another way.

All of us have to realize that there is such a fact that our spirit is mingled with God's Spirit. We have to realize this is a fact which has been wrought into our being. This is a fact which is wrapped up with our innermost being. This is a big involvement and a big complication. (*Perfecting Training,* pp. 582-583)

Further Reading: Life-study of 1 Corinthians, msgs. 12, 16, 39; *The Experience and Growth in Life,* msg. 20; *Life-study of John,* msg. 9; *Basic Training,* msg. 5; *Life-study of Colossians,* msg. 52; *The Divine Dispensing of the Divine Trinity,* ch. 28

Enlightenment and inspiration: _____

_____

_____

_____

Morning Nourishment

1 Cor. **And God has both raised up the Lord and will raise**
6:14-15 **us up through His power. Do you not know that**
your bodies are members of Christ?...
   17 **But he who is joined to the Lord is one spirit.**
19-20 **Or do you not know that your body is a temple of the**
Holy Spirit within you, whom you have from God,
and you are not your own? For you have been bought
with a price. So then glorify God in your body.

Notice that [in 1 Corinthians 6:15] Paul does not say merely that we are members of Christ; he declares that our bodies are members of Christ. The subject of these verses is the abuse of freedom in foods and in the body. Thus, Paul's concern is the believers' body.

Because we are organically united with Christ and because Christ dwells in our spirit (2 Tim. 4:22) and makes His home in our heart (Eph. 3:17), our entire being, including our purified body, becomes a member of Him. Verse 17 indicates that we are organically united with Christ. To be one spirit with the Lord is to enter into an organic union with Him, to be united with Him organically. This organic union makes it possible for our bodies to be the members of Christ. Christ indwells our spirit, and from our spirit spreads throughout our inner being, thereby making His home in our hearts. Furthermore, according to Romans 8:11, from our inner being He seeks to impart Himself as life into our physical body. Therefore, Christ spreads from the spirit to the soul and from the soul to the body. In this way our bodies become His members. (*Life-study of 1 Corinthians,* pp. 356-357)

Today's Reading

In 1 Corinthians 6:15, 17, and 19 Paul covers three crucial matters: that our bodies are the members of Christ; that we are joined to the Lord as one spirit; and that our body is a temple of the Holy Spirit. In actuality and practicality these three are one. The key to all three is in verse 17. Apart from being joined to the Lord in our spirit, it is impossible for our bodies, which are sinful and lustful, to become the members of Christ. Another crucial matter related to this is Paul's word in 6:14 that the Lord "will raise us up through His power." We have pointed out that even now the Spirit of the resurrected Christ who dwells in our spirit gives life to our body. This impartation of life makes our bodies the members of Christ and a temple of the Holy Spirit. Have you ever wondered how our bodies can become the members of Christ and the temple of the Holy Spirit? The key is that the indwelling Spirit of the resurrected Christ imparts life into our mortal bodies.

Since this is the key, we must exercise and practice to experience the Lord as the life-giving Spirit dwelling in our spirit. This is to practice being one spirit with the Lord. If we exercise ourselves to experience this and enjoy it, we shall open the door for the Lord to impart life to our physical bodies. Then our bodies will be full of the resurrection life of Christ and will become the members of Christ. When our body becomes a member of the indwelling Christ, it automatically becomes the temple, the dwelling place, of the Holy Spirit. Therefore, in our experience the three matters of our bodies being members of Christ, of being one spirit with the Lord, and of our body being the temple of the Holy Spirit are three aspects of one reality.

The way Paul deals with the problems among the Corinthian believers is not shallow or superficial. On the contrary, it is deep and profound. As Paul deals with the different problems, he brings us back to the central vision of God's economy—to the Triune God as the all-inclusive life-giving Spirit dwelling in our spirit. The Spirit today is the processed Triune God indwelling our whole being. All the problems among the believers are caused by the shortage of the experience of this indwelling Spirit. (*Life-study of 1 Corinthians,* pp. 357-358)

Further Reading: Life-study of 1 Corinthians, msgs. 12, 16, 40; *The Completing Ministry of Paul,* ch. 7; *The Central Line of the Divine Revelation,* msg. 17; *Messages to the Trainees in Fall 1990,* chs. 8-9; *Life Lessons,* lsn. 30

Enlightenment and inspiration: _____

_____

_____

Morning Nourishment

1 Cor. 6:17 But he who is joined to the Lord is one spirit.

Rom. 8:16 The Spirit Himself witnesses with our spirit that we are children of God.

John 1:13 Who were begotten not of blood, nor of the will of the flesh, nor of the will of man, but of God.

3:6 That which is born of the flesh is flesh, and that which is born of the Spirit is spirit.

Phil. 1:21 For to me, to live is Christ...

Today, the Spirit of God and the human spirit are mingled as one within us so that we can live a God-man life, a life that is God yet man and man yet God. Hence, the God-man life is a living of the two spirits, the Spirit of God and the spirit of man joined and mingled together as one. (*The Issue of the Union of the Consummated Spirit of the Triune God and the Regenerated Spirit of the Believers*, p. 30)

Today's Reading

In this message we do not want to merely repeat the items of God's organic salvation. Instead, we want to see that the key of God's organic salvation is the Spirit Himself with our spirit. We should not forget that there is such a marvelous phrase in the Bible in Romans 8:16. Even after we enter into the New Jerusalem, I would like to see a banner there, saying—"The Spirit Himself with our spirit." The Spirit Himself with our spirit is doing one thing: witnessing that we are the children of God. Just to say *the people of God* is not too critical, but to say *the children of God* is so great.

The Spirit Himself is the witnessing One, and this Spirit is the Spirit of life, the Spirit who gives life, the Spirit who is the Spirit of Christ. This Spirit is also the pneumatic Christ and the indwelling Spirit. Our spirit was created by God but became dead through the fall. But later it was regenerated by God. Not only so, after regeneration the regenerating Spirit remains in our regenerated spirit and mingles Himself with our spirit to make the two one. First Corinthians 6:17

says, "He who is joined to the Lord is one spirit."

Not only are we God-men but also we are one with God, one spirit with God. The human spirit and the divine Spirit are not only joined and mingled but are also one spirit. The Spirit is life and the One who gives life. God is the Spirit and in His marvelous organic salvation, He has made us one spirit with Him. This is just a simple word in 1 Corinthians 6:17, but I never saw this truth until after I had studied the Bible for at least thirty years. One day I realized that I am one spirit with God. This is not a small thing. Regretfully, even in the Lord's recovery, many of the elders and even the co-workers do not know their real status. Our real status is that we are one spirit with God. We have been saved to such a high level. What God is, we are.

When we realize our status, this will affect our living. When I speak with others in a joking way, I am inwardly rebuked for being so loose and light with no gravity. I am reminded about my status, and I have to confess to the Lord. Due to my divine status, I dare not be loose or light. I dare not joke. Even with my grandchildren I dare not speak lightly, because I am not merely their grandfather. I am a grandfather who has the same status as God.

According to 1 Corinthians 6:17 God's intention in His organic salvation is to join the believer's spirit with His Spirit as one spirit—a mingled spirit. Eventually, this is not just the mingled spirit but a spirit that is one spirit with God, that is the same as God in His life and nature but not in His Godhead. This is the key to open the eight sections of the organic salvation of God. If we do not have this key, the door is closed. When we have this key, the door is open and we can see all things concealed within. (*The Divine and Mystical Realm,* pp. 53-54)

Further Reading: The Issue of the Union of the Consummated
   Spirit of the Triune God and the Regenerated Spirit of the
   Believers, chs. 2-3; The Divine and Mystical Realm, ch. 4

Enlightenment and inspiration: _____

_____

_____

_____

Morning Nourishment

1 Cor. However as the Lord has apportioned to each one,
7:17 as God has called each one, so let him walk. And
so I direct in all the churches.
20-21 Each one, in the calling in which he was called, in
this let him remain. Were you called as a slave? Let
it not concern you; but even if you are able to
become free, use *your status as a slave* rather.
24 Each one, brothers, in what *status* he was called,
in this let him remain with God.

Paul was not only absolute for the Lord, but he was also
absolutely one with God. Because Paul was one with God, he
answered the questions in such a way that the Corinthians
would be helped to be one with Him in every circumstance,
condition, and situation. We know this by the fact that in
answering certain questions Paul followed the principle of not
initiating anything or changing anything. He made it very clear
to the Corinthians that they should not initiate any action or
change their status in any way.

It is important to see this principle of being absolutely one
with the Lord in all circumstances, situations, and conditions.
If we are mindful of this principle as we read 1 Corinthians 7,
we shall see that Paul is utterly one with the Lord and that in
his instructions and answers he spontaneously and unconsciously expresses such an absolute spirit. Because Paul had
this kind of spirit, he could answer the Corinthians' questions
in a clear and absolute way, in a way that would help them also
to become one with God in their situation. (*Life-study of 1 Corinthians,* pp. 371, 373)

Today's Reading

Another very important point revealed in this chapter is that
those who love the Lord, who are for Him, and who are one with
Him must be willing to accept any kind of circumstance or
situation. For example, if a brother's unbelieving wife desires
to remain with him, he should accept this situation. But if she

decides to leave, he should also accept this circumstance.

It is very important for us to see that God is always in our circumstances. We may say that the circumstances are actually God coming to us in disguise. Apparently we are in a particular circumstance; actually that circumstance is God coming to us and God with us....Notice the words "with God" [in verse 24]. They indicate that when we take our circumstances we take God. Both within the circumstances and behind them, God is present.

Paul had an excellent spirit, a spirit which was submissive, content, and satisfied. Paul did not have any complaints. In his spirit he was very submissive and content with his situation. No matter how he was treated, he did not complain. To him, every situation was of the Lord, and he would not initiate anything to change it. Paul could say, "To me, everything works for good. This is the reason I don't want to change anything. I know that when I take my circumstances, I take my God. In every situation is my God, the One whom I love and the One to whom I belong absolutely." What an excellent spirit is displayed in this attitude!

The way we answer others or respond to a situation always indicates the kind of spirit we have. Suppose a brother is very happy in the morning. When his wife calls him for breakfast, he says, "Praise the Lord!" His response reveals his spirit. But suppose his spirit is heavy....He may respond in a very different way....His reaction may indicate that he is unhappy with his wife and that he has a problem with the Lord. The principle here is that our answers and responses always express our spirit.

I appreciate 1 Corinthians 7 not primarily for all the answers it gives but because this chapter conveys the spirit of a person who loves the Lord, who cares for the Lord's interests on earth, who is absolutely for the Lord and one with the Lord, and who in every respect is obedient, submissive, and satisfied with God and the circumstances arranged by Him. (*Life-study of 1 Corinthians,* pp. 374-375)

Further Reading: Life-study of 1 Corinthians, msg. 42

Enlightenment and inspiration: _____

_____
_____
_____

Morning Nourishment

John   Abide in Me and I in you. As the branch cannot
15:4-5   bear fruit of itself unless it abides in the vine, so
          neither *can* you unless you abide in Me. I am the
          vine; you are the branches. He who abides in Me
          and I in him, he bears much fruit; for apart from
          Me you can do nothing.
1 Cor.   But to the rest I say, I, not the Lord, If any brother
7:12   has an unbelieving wife and she consents to dwell
          with him, he must not leave her.

The Christian life is a life in the principle of incarnation....As Christians we have a dual nature. We are no longer
merely men. We are God-men. Before the incarnation of Jesus,
the New Testament had not come into being....The incarnation
of Jesus initiated and ushered in the New Testament. Now we,
the New Testament believers, are wonderful persons who have
God in us and have been made one with God. How glorious it
is to be one with God, to be a God-man.

In the Old Testament, when the prophets prophesied for God,
...the word of Jehovah came objectively upon the speakers, and
they declared that it was not their word but the Lord's. However,
in 1 Corinthians 7:25 Paul said, "Now concerning virgins I have
no commandment of the Lord, but I give my opinion as one who
has been shown mercy by the Lord to be faithful"; and in giving
his opinion he said, "But I think that I also have the Spirit of
God" (7:40). Paul indicated that what he spoke was not a word
from the Lord; it was his opinion. Yet in the giving of his opinion
was the speaking of God. God lived in Paul and spoke in Paul's
speaking, even in his opinion, because God had become one with
Paul and had made Paul one with Him. While we are speaking,
it is not only we but Christ, the embodiment of God, who speaks
with us and speaks in our speaking. This is the principle of
incarnation. (*The Experience and Growth in Life,* pp. 201-202)

Today's Reading

First Corinthians 7 is mysterious and deep. In this chapter

Paul never utters the words, "Thus says the Lord." The reason Paul does not use such an expression is that the apostles' teaching in the New Testament is altogether based on the principle of incarnation. According to this principle, God speaks in man's speaking. When the Lord Jesus spoke, it was difficult for others to discern who was speaking. To be sure, it was a man who was speaking....When the Lord Jesus spoke to the Pharisees, it seems that He was an ordinary person from Nazareth. There was no indication that He was different, and the Pharisees regarded Him as a man without learning. But the Lord Jesus is God incarnate. With Him there is the reality of incarnation. Thus, while He was speaking, God spoke also. Actually, His speaking was God's speaking. God spoke with Him. This means that in the Lord Jesus God and man spoke together as one. This is the principle of incarnation.

On the day of Pentecost the apostles and disciples also began to speak according to the principle of incarnation. This is the reason the writings of Peter, John, and Paul recorded in the Bible could become God's words. Furthermore, these words are among the contents of the New Testament. Although Paul writes in 1 Corinthians 7 that certain things he says are not the Lord's word or the Lord's commandment, everything spoken by Paul in this chapter has nonetheless become part of the divine revelation in the New Testament. This is because Paul was a person absolutely one with God. Even when he says that he does not have a word from the Lord, the Lord speaks in his speaking. Because Paul was one with the Lord, when he spoke, the Lord spoke with him. Thus, with Paul in 1 Corinthians 7 we have an example of the principle of incarnation. It is very important that we see this principle and understand it. (*Life-study of 1 Corinthians,* pp. 378-379)

Further Reading: The Experience and Growth in Life, msgs. 25, 29, 31; Life-study of 1 Corinthians, msg. 43; Elders' Training, Book 6: The Crucial Points of the Truth in Paul's Epistles, ch. 3

Enlightenment and inspiration: _____

Morning Nourishment

1 Cor. But to the married I charge, not I but the Lord, A
7:10 wife must not be separated from *her* husband.
  25 Now concerning virgins I have no commandment
of the Lord, but I give *my* opinion as one who has
been shown mercy by the Lord to be faithful.
  40 But she is more blessed if she so remains, according to my opinion; but I think that I also have the
Spirit of God.
Gal. I am crucified with Christ; and *it is* no longer I *who*
2:20 live, but *it is* Christ *who* lives in me...

We have seen that the Old Testament principle of speaking
for God, of prophesying, is, "Thus says the Lord" (Isa. 10:24; 50:1;
Jer. 2:2; Ezek. 2:4). But the New Testament principle of incarnation is "I charge" [1 Cor. 7:10]; that is, the speaker charges.
The speaker and the Lord are one. Hence, Paul also says, "Not
I but the Lord." The Greek word for *charge* may also be translated enjoin or command.

The words "I charge, not I but the Lord," indicate two things:
first, that the apostle is one with the Lord; hence, what he
commands, the Lord commands. Second, his commandments
are the Lord's. What Paul commands here the Lord had already
commanded in Matthew 5:31-32 and 19:3-9. Divorce is altogether not allowed by the Lord. The principle in 1 Corinthians
7:10 is the same as that in Galatians 2:20, where Paul says, "It
is no longer I who live, but it is Christ who lives in me." In both
verses we see the principle of incarnation—two persons living
as one person. In 7:10 we have two persons, the Lord and Paul,
speaking as one. (*Life-study of 1 Corinthians,* pp. 379-380)

Today's Reading

A wife should not be separated from her husband. This, the
apostle says, is the Lord's commandment (v. 10). But concerning
virgins not marrying, he says he has no commandment of the
Lord, but he gives his opinion in the following verses [v. 25]. He

dares to do this because he has received mercy of the Lord to be faithful to the Lord's interests, and he is really one with the Lord. His opinion expresses the Lord's desire. This is again based on the New Testament principle of incarnation.

Some readers of 1 Corinthians may think that Paul was too strong in giving his opinion when he had no commandment from the Lord....Yet this is the very thing Paul does in verse 25. Here we see the highest spirituality, the spirituality of a person who is so one with the Lord that even his opinion expresses the Lord's mind. Paul was absolutely one with the Lord and thoroughly saturated with Him. Because his entire being was permeated with the Lord, even his opinion expressed the mind of the Lord. For this reason, we say that verse 25 expresses the highest spirituality.

In the New Testament the Lord becomes one with His apostles and they become one with Him. Both speak together. His word becomes their word, and whatever they utter is His word. Hence, the apostle's charge is the Lord's charge (v. 10). What he says, though not by the Lord, still becomes a part of the divine revelation in the New Testament (v. 12). He is so one with the Lord that even when he gives his own opinion, not the commandment of the Lord (v. 25), he still thinks that he also has the Spirit of God [v. 40]. He does not claim definitely to have the Spirit of God, but he *thinks* that he *also* has the Spirit of God. This is the highest spirituality; it is based on the principle of incarnation.

We need to see the principle of incarnation illustrated here and receive mercy and grace from the Lord to speak in a genuine and frank manner without any pretense. In order to speak like this we need to be saturated with the Spirit. Then what we utter or express will be our thought, our opinion, but it will also be something of the Lord because we are one with Him. (*Life-study of 1 Corinthians,* pp. 381-383)

Further Reading: Life-study of 1 Corinthians, msg. 43; *The Experience and Growth in Life,* msgs. 25, 29, 31; *The Divine Dispensing of the Divine Trinity,* ch. 28*

Enlightenment and inspiration: _____

_____

_____

_____

Hymns, #782

1   How mysterious, O Lord,
      That Thy Spirit dwells in mine;
      O how marvelous it is,
      Into one, two spirits twine.

2   By the spirit I can walk,
      Spiritual in spirit be;
      By the spirit I can serve,
      And in spirit worship Thee.

3   Thru Thy Word and by my prayer
      In the spirit touching Thee,
      Lifted high my spirit is,
      Strengthened shall my spirit be.

4   Make my spirit strong I pray
      Others' spirits to revive;
      Lift my spirit high and free,
      Others' spirits then may thrive.

5   Every time I speak, O Lord,
      May my spirit actuate;
      And whatever I may do,
      Let my spirit motivate.

6   Every time my spirit acts
      Others' spirits opened be,
      Every time my spirit moves
      Others' lifted unto Thee.

7   Lord, have mercy, from above
      May Thy Spirit breathe on me;
      Then my spirit will be rich,
      Strengthened and refreshed by Thee.

Composition for prophecy with main point and sub-points: _____

_____

_____

_____

_____

_____

_____

_____

_____

_____

_____

_____

_____

_____

_____

_____

_____

_____

_____

_____

_____

_____

_____

_____

_____

_____

_____

_____

_____

_____

_____

_____

_____

_____

_____

The Kingdom Reward and
the Universal Headship

Scripture Reading: 1 Cor. 9:24-27; 3:10-17;10:1-13; 11:2-3, 10;
15:22-28

Day 1 I. **The Christian life is a race that we must run
successfully to obtain the prize, the kingdom
reward (9:24; Heb. 12:1):**

A. Paul began to run the heavenly race after the
Lord took possession of him, and he continually
ran that he might finish it (1 Cor. 9:24-27; Phil.
3:12-14; Acts 20:24).

B. At the end Paul triumphantly proclaimed, "I
have finished the course," and for this he received from the Lord a reward—the crown of
righteousness (2 Tim. 4:6-8):

1. The incorruptible crown, the crown of righteousness, which the Lord will award to His
overcoming saints who win the race, is a
reward in addition to salvation; in contrast
to the salvation which is of grace and by faith
(Eph. 2:5, 8-9), this prize is of righteousness
through works (Matt. 16:27; Rev. 22:12;
2 Cor. 5:10).

2. Whether we will be rewarded by Him depends upon how we run the race; in view of
this prize the apostle charged the Corinthian
believers to run the race that they might
obtain the reward (1 Cor. 9:24).

3. The uttermost enjoyment of Christ in the
millennial kingdom will be a reward to the
victorious runners of the New Testament
race (Phil. 3:14).

Day 2 C. Paul was very much on the alert to run his
course by subduing his body to serve his holy
purpose, that he might not be disapproved
and rejected at the judgment seat of Christ and

be found unworthy of the reward of the kingdom (1 Cor. 9:24-27; Matt. 7:21-23; 25:11-12):

1. We need to subdue our body and make it a
   conquered captive to serve us as a slave for
   fulfilling our holy purpose.

2. This is equivalent to putting to death our
   earthly members (Col. 3:5) and putting to
   death the practices of the body (Rom. 8:13),
   not allowing our body to be used for the
   indulgence of lust or doing anything on our
   own except what is holy to God (1 Cor. 6:19-
   20; 10:31).

Day 3   D. We need to be encouraged and warned by the
   type of the children of Israel, whose journey
   toward the good land typifies the Christian race
   toward our good land, the all-inclusive Christ
   (vv. 1-13):

1. Although we have been redeemed through
   Christ, delivered out of Satan's bondage, and
   brought into the revelation of God's economy,
   we may yet fail to reach the goal of God's
   calling, that is, to enter into the possession of
   our good land, Christ (Phil. 3:12-14), and enjoy
   His riches for the kingdom of God that we may
   be His expression in the present age and
   participate in the fullest enjoyment of Christ
   in the kingdom age (Matt. 25:21, 23).

2. We need to run with endurance the race which
   is set before us, looking away unto Jesus, the
   Author and Perfecter of our faith (Heb. 12:1-2a).

Day 4   E. In order to receive the kingdom reward, we
   must take heed how we build the church, that
   is, with what materials we build the church
   (1 Cor. 3:10-17):

1. If we build with gold (God's nature), silver
   (Christ's redemptive work), and precious
   stones (the Spirit's transforming work), we
   will receive a reward (vv. 12, 14).

2. If we build with wood (human nature), grass (man in the flesh), and stubble (lifelessness), we will be saved, yet so as through fire (v. 15).

3. To build with the worthless materials of wood, grass, and stubble is to corrupt, ruin, defile, mar, and destroy the temple of God (v. 17).

4. All those who have corrupted, ruined, defiled, and marred the church of God by their heretical doctrines, divisive teachings, worldly ways, and natural efforts in building will suffer God's punishment; since the temple of God, the church, is holy, the materials, the ways, and the efforts by which we build it also must be holy.

5. As God's fellow workers, working together with Him (John 5:17; 1 Cor. 3:9; 2 Cor. 6:1), we must be faithful stewards of the mysteries of God (1 Cor. 4:1-2; 7:25; 9:17; 1 Pet. 4:10; cf. Num. 18:1):

   a. The initiation of God's work must be out of God and not out of us (Rom. 11:36).

   b. The advance of God's work must be by God's power and not by our power (Acts 1:8; Zech. 4:6).

   c. The result of God's work must be for God's glory and not for our glory (John 7:18; Eph. 3:21).

Day 5 II. We need to honor the headship of Christ and of God in the divine government—"I want you to know that Christ is the head of every man, and the man is the head of the woman, and God is the head of Christ" (1 Cor. 11:3; cf. 15:22-28):

A. Here the headship of Christ over every man is related to individuals; Christ is the Head of the Body, the church (Eph. 5:23), corporately, and of the believers individually.

B. Trying to assume headship without first coming under God's headship was the cause of the fall of the angels; we want to testify to the rebellious angels that we accept Christ as our Head (Isa. 14:12-15; 1 Cor. 11:2-3, 10).

C. God's goal is to appoint Christ as the Head so that every man would submit to Him; we must be a people under God's headship, reflecting through our own submission to Christ His own submission to God (Eph. 1:10; 1 Cor. 11:10).

Day 6

D. Christ, the Son of God, as the Head of mankind in His humanity, is under the headship of God the Father for the government of God's kingdom:

1. After God the Father has subjected all things under the feet of Christ as a resurrected man in glory (Eph. 1:22; Heb. 2:7-8), and after Christ as such a resurrected man has put all enemies under His feet to execute God the Father's subjection of all things to Him, He as the Son of God, along with His delivering of the kingdom back to God the Father, will also subject Himself in His divinity to God, who has subjected all things to Him, the Son in His humanity (1 Cor. 15:24-28).

2. This indicates the Son's absolute subjection and subordination to the Father, which exalts the Father that God the Father may be all in all.

Morning Nourishment

1 Cor. And I do all things for the sake of the gospel that I
9:23-25 may become a fellow partaker of it. Do you not know
that those who run on a racecourse all run, but one
receives the prize? Run in this way, that you may lay
hold. And everyone who contends exercises self-
control in all things; they then, that they may receive a corruptible crown, but we, an incorruptible.
2 Tim. I have fought the good fight; I have finished the
4:7-8 course; I have kept the faith. Henceforth there is
laid up for me the crown of righteousness, with
which the Lord, the righteous Judge, will recompense me in that day, and not only me but also all
those who have loved His appearing.

I do ask you to reverently consider this matter. Paul said that
all run in the race, but only one receives the prize. Then he said
that we should run in such a way to receive the reward (1 Cor. 9:24).
At the end of Paul's life he said that he had fought the good fight,
finished the course, and kept the faith. He testified that there was
a crown of righteousness prepared for him (2 Tim. 4:7-8). I hope
that when we end this life, we could say that we have done the
same thing. (*The Practical Points concerning Blending*, p. 47)

Today's Reading

[First Corinthians 9:24] reveals that the Christian life is a
race we must run successfully. The prize is a reward as an
incentive. To lay hold is to obtain the prize.

Actually verse 24 should not be separated from verse 23, for
verse 24 is the explanation of what it means to be a fellow
partaker of the gospel, as mentioned in verse 23. To run in a
racecourse is to labor, but to receive the prize is to have enjoyment. As we preach the gospel today, we are running the course.
But to receive a reward, a prize, at the coming of the Lord is to
have a particular enjoyment.

In 9:17 Paul speaks of a reward. In Acts 20:24 he refers to

the course: "But I consider my life of no account as if precious to myself, in order that I may finish my course and the ministry which I have received from the Lord Jesus to solemnly testify of the gospel of the grace of God." Paul regarded his preaching of the gospel as the running of the Christian race. [First Corinthians 9:24] indicates that all believers are running a race. Here Paul exhorts us to run so that we may obtain, lay hold of, the prize.

We have seen that the Christian course involves the preaching of the gospel. To preach the gospel is to dispense Christ into God's chosen ones....If a person receives our preaching, this proves that he has been chosen by God. We should dispense Christ into such receptive ones. In this way we run the Christian course. However, because many believers today are not running the race, we need Paul's word, "Run in this way, that you may lay hold."

In verse 25 Paul continues....All those who contend in the games, Paul says, exercise strict self-control....If athletes exercise self-control in order to receive a corruptible crown, we should exercise self-control even more to obtain an incorruptible crown.

This incorruptible crown, which the Lord will award His overcoming saints who win the race, is a reward in addition to salvation. As believers, we have all received His salvation through faith in Him. This has been settled once for all. But whether we shall be rewarded by Him depends on how we run the race. Here in this chapter the apostle is running the course. In Philippians, one of his last Epistles, he was still running (Phil. 3:14). It was not until the last moment of his running, in 2 Timothy 4:6-8, that Paul had the assurance that he would be rewarded by the Lord at His appearing. With this prize in view, the apostle charged the Corinthian believers to run the race that they might obtain the reward. (*Life-study of 1 Corinthians,* pp. 410-411)

Further Reading: The Practical Points concerning Blending, ch. 5; *Life-study of 1 Corinthians,* msg. 46; *Elders' Training, Book 6: The Crucial Points of the Truth in Paul's Epistles,* ch. 3

Enlightenment and inspiration: _____

_____
_____
_____

Morning Nourishment

1 Cor. I therefore run in this way, not as though without
9:26-27 a clear aim; I box in this way, not as though beating
the air; but I buffet my body and make *it* my slave,
lest perhaps having preached to others, I myself
may become disapproved.

Matt. Not every one who says to Me, Lord, Lord, will enter
7:21-23 into the kingdom of the heavens, but he who does the
will of My Father who is in the heavens. Many will
say to Me in that day, Lord, Lord, *was it* not in Your
name *that* we prophesied, and in Your name cast out
demons, and in Your name did many works of power?
And then I will declare to them: I never knew you.
Depart from Me, you workers of lawlessness.

The Greek word translated *buffet* [in 1 Corinthians 9:27]
literally means "to beat the face under the eye black and blue."
This is not to ill-treat the body as in asceticism, nor to consider
the body evil as in Gnosticism. This is to subdue the body and
make it a conquered captive to serve as a slave for fulfilling our
holy purpose. It is the equivalent of putting to death our earthly
members (Col. 3:5) and putting to death the practices of the body
(Rom. 8:13), not allowing our body to be used for the indulgence
of lust nor doing anything on our own except what is holy to
God. The Corinthians misused their body by indulgence in
fornication, not caring for God's temple (1 Cor. 6:19), and in the
unrestrained eating of sacrifices to idols, not caring for weak
believers (8:9-13). (*Life-study of 1 Corinthians*, pp. 411-412)

Today's Reading

Paul also tells us that he makes his body his slave. This is a
metaphor which means…to bring the captive into slavery and
make him a slave to serve the conqueror's purpose.…This indicates that we need to conquer our body and subdue it. Our body
has been captured by lusts. Now we must deliver it and bring it
into captivity, into a very positive kind of slavery where our body
becomes the temple of the Holy Spirit and a member of Christ.

According to 1 Corinthians 9:27, Paul was concerned lest having preached to others, he himself would become disapproved.... The Greek word rendered *disapproved* also means "disqualified," "rejected," that is, "unworthy of the prize." The apostle was surely saved by grace through faith in Christ. Not only so, he was also called to be an apostle to carry out God's New Testament economy. Nonetheless, in verse 27 he is very much on the alert to run his course (Acts 20:24) by subduing his body to serve his holy purpose, lest he be disapproved and rejected at the judgment seat of Christ (2 Cor. 5:10) and be found unworthy of the reward of the coming kingdom.

The judgment which will take place at the judgment seat of Christ will determine whether we are approved by the Lord or disapproved, whether we shall be known by the Lord or be rejected by Him. In Matthew 7:22 the Lord Jesus says that on that day many will tell the Lord that they prophesied in His name, cast out demons in His name, and did many mighty works in His name. However, the Lord will say that He never knew them (v. 23). This means that He does not approve of what they have done. Their Christian life was not a pleasure or joy to Him. On the contrary, their work was done presumptuously according to their own will and choice. Therefore, instead of approving them, the Lord rejects them as far as the reward in the coming kingdom is concerned. Paul was afraid lest having preached the gospel regarding the reward to others, he himself would be disapproved by the Lord.

First Corinthians 9 reveals Paul's faithfulness. In his spirit he was utterly faithful to the Lord's charge and commission. The Lord had charged him to run the course, and he was endeavoring to run it. We also need to run the Christian course in such a way that we shall not be disapproved, rejected, disqualified, from the enjoyment in the coming kingdom as a reward. (*Life-study of 1 Corinthians*, pp. 412-413)

Further Reading: Life-study of 1 Corinthians, msg. 46

Enlightenment and inspiration: _____

_____

_____

_____

Morning Nourishment

1 Cor. But with most of them God was not well pleased,
10:5-6 for they were strewn along in the wilderness. Now these things occurred as examples to us, that we should not be ones who lust after evil things, even as they also lusted.

 11 Now these things happened to them as an example, and they were written for our admonition, unto whom the ends of the ages have come.

Phil. Brothers, I do not account of myself to have laid hold;
3:13-14 but one thing *I do:* Forgetting the things which are behind and stretching forward to the things which are before, I pursue toward the goal for the prize to which God in Christ Jesus has called *me* upward.

In the first section of the history of Israel every positive thing is a type of Christ or of something related to Christ....But the ultimate type of Christ, the greatest and all-inclusive type, is the good land. The children of Israel entered the good land, possessed it, and enjoyed it. We need to apply this part of their history to our experience today.

As we consider this portion of their history, we shall see that the children of Israel were not defeated. On the contrary, they were victorious: they gained the land, entered it, possessed it, and enjoyed it. This should encourage us not to be disappointed by the situation among Christians today. We must believe that our God is still the God of victory and that He has a way to carry out His purpose. Furthermore, we also believe that the recovery is needed for God to fulfill what is typified by that portion of the history of Israel concerned with entering the land, possessing it, and enjoying it. (*Life-study of 1 Corinthians,* pp. 431-432)

Today's Reading

In 1 Corinthians 10:6...Paul says that these things happened as examples to us. Thus, he includes himself with all believers in the matter of running the Christian race. These examples indicate that we should not be lusters after evil things, as the children of Israel lusted. The word *also* in verse 6 indicates that the Corinthians were lusting after evil things. Therefore, Paul warns them not to be those who lust.

We have seen that 1 Corinthians takes the history of the children of Israel in the Old Testament as a type of the New Testament believers. In chapters five, seven, and eight they have experienced Christ as their Passover and have begun to keep the feast of unleavened bread. Here in this chapter they have been baptized unto their Moses (Christ)....They are now eating the spiritual food and drinking the spiritual drink that they may take their journey (the Christian race) toward their good land (the all-inclusive Christ). They are also warned here (v. 11) not to repeat the history of the children of Israel in doing evil against God, as illustrated in verses 6 through 11.

The goal of God's calling the children of Israel was to enter into the promised land to enjoy its riches that they might establish God's kingdom and be God's expression on earth. However, although all had been redeemed through the Passover, delivered out of the Egyptian tyranny, and brought to the mountain of God to receive the revelation of God's dwelling place, the tabernacle, nearly all fell and died in the wilderness, failing to reach this goal (Heb. 3:7-19) because of their evil doings and unbelief. Only Caleb and Joshua made it into the good land (Num. 14:27-30). This signifies that although we have been redeemed through Christ, delivered out of Satan's bondage, and brought into the revelation of God's economy, we may yet fail to reach the goal of God's calling, that is, to enter into the possession of our good land, Christ (Phil. 3:12-14), and enjoy His riches for the kingdom of God that we may be His expression in the present age and participate in the fullest enjoyment of Christ in the kingdom age (Matt. 25:21, 23). This should be a solemn warning to all New Testament believers. (*Life-study of 1 Corinthians,* pp. 421-422)

Further Reading: Life-study of 1 Corinthians, msgs. 47-48

Enlightenment and inspiration: _____

_____

_____

_____

Morning Nourishment

1 Cor. For another foundation no one is able to lay be-
3:11-12 sides that which is laid, which is Jesus Christ. But
         if anyone builds upon the foundation gold, silver,
         precious stones, wood, grass, stubble.
  14-15 If anyone's work which he has built upon *the
         foundation* remains, he will receive a reward; if
         anyone's work is consumed, he will suffer loss, but
         he himself will be saved, yet so as through fire.
     17 If anyone destroys the temple of God, God will
         destroy him; for the temple of God is holy, *and
         such are you.*

The proper building materials for the church are gold, silver,
and precious stones (1 Cor. 3:12a). Gold symbolizes the divine
nature of God the Father. Silver symbolizes Christ's redemptive
work. Precious stones symbolize the Spirit's transforming work.
This indicates that what we build upon the foundation of Christ
should be something of the Triune God—the Father, the Son,
and the Spirit.

We should not build the church with wood, grass, and stubble
(1 Cor. 3:12b). Just as gold signifies God's nature, wood signifies
the human nature. Grass signifies man in the flesh (Isa. 40:6-7).
Stubble signifies lifelessness. Stubble is the stump of the crops
after being reaped. With the stubble there is no seed, no life. We
have to admit that most of the work in Christianity is according
to and out of these three negative items—the human nature,
the human flesh, and lifelessness.

In verses 14 and 15, both reward and salvation are mentioned.
The reward is not for salvation. Neither can salvation replace the
reward. If our work...is really of gold, silver, and precious stone,
it can stand the test of fire. These materials will not be burned.
If our work is with these materials, we will receive a reward....Ap-
parently speaking, [the reward in the coming age] will be an
entering into the manifestation of the kingdom of the heavens,
but our entering the kingdom is for the greater, higher, and richer
enjoyment of Christ. (*Basic Lessons on Service*, pp. 122-124)

Today's Reading

First Corinthians 3:17 warns us not to destroy the temple of God. *Destroy* in Greek means "ruin, corrupt, defile, mar." To build with the worthless materials of wood, grass, and stubble is to destroy the temple of God. If anyone destroys the temple of God, God will destroy him....In these seventy years I have seen clearly that those who have damaged the Body of Christ have all suffered serious consequences and were destroyed by God. This is a serious matter.

Today we are here not to destroy the Body of Christ; rather, we are adorning it. I dare not bring my flesh with me to build the New Jerusalem, that is to destroy the New Jerusalem. I dare not bring my opinions, my old "I," my preferences, and my views to build the New Jerusalem. I simply want to be in fear and trembling to adorn the divine building with God the Father as the pure gold, God the Son as the pearl, and God the Spirit for the wall of precious stones. All of us must have this kind of attitude in our living.

In the past there was a large frame in my study in which these words were written: "...he himself will be saved, yet so as through fire" (1 Cor. 3:15). If you build the temple of God with gold, silver, and precious stones, you will receive a reward. However, if you build with wood, grass, and stubble, your work will be consumed, but you yourself will be saved, yet so as through fire....I hung that portion of 1 Corinthians on the wall in my home so that I might always be reminded....Whenever we touch the eternal goal of God, the New Jerusalem, we need to be very pure; we must not be careless. (*How to Be a Co-worker and an Elder and How to Fulfill Their Obligations,* pp. 88-90)

Further Reading: Basic Lessons on Service, lsn. 15; *How to Be a Co-worker and an Elder and How to Fulfill Their Obligations,* ch. 6; *The Collected Works of Watchman Nee,* vol. 42, ch. 45; *Crystallization-study of Song of Songs,* msg. 4

Enlightenment and inspiration: _____

_____

_____

_____

Morning Nourishment

1 Cor. But I want you to know that Christ is the head of
11:3   every man, and the man is the head of the woman,
        and God is the head of Christ.
Eph.   Unto the economy of the fullness of the times, to
1:10   head up all things in Christ, the things in the
        heavens and the things on the earth, in Him.
5:23   For a husband is head of the wife as also Christ is
        Head of the church, He Himself *being* the Savior
        of the Body.

First Corinthians 11:3 through 16 deals with the...problem concerning head covering....[Head covering] is concerning the headship of Christ and of God in the divine government. In Ephesians 1:22 and 23 the headship of Christ over all things is to His Body, the church. Here the headship of Christ over every man is concerning individuals. Christ is both the Head corporately of the Body, the church, and individually of the believers. He is the Head directly of every one of us. In the apostle's dealing with the Corinthians' problems concerning God's administration, this matter of the headship of Christ and of God is his first concern.

In verse 3 Paul points out that the head of the woman is the man. In the divine governmental ordination, woman is under the headship of man. God created the female in this way (Gen. 2:18-24; 1 Tim. 2:13). According to the nature (1 Cor. 11:14) created by God, woman is subordinate to man.

Paul also says in verse 3 that the head of Christ is God. Christ is God's anointed One, appointed by God. Hence, He is under God, and God as the originator is His Head. This refers to the relationship between Christ and God in the divine government. (*Life-study of 1 Corinthians*, pp. 469-470)

Today's Reading

We need to link Paul's word about head covering in 11:2-16 to the entire book of Revelation....According to Revelation 4 and 5, in the heavens, before the throne of God, there is no rebellion. Instead, as we have pointed out, the slain, resurrected, and ascended Lamb is taking the lead to submit Himself to the headship of God in the heavens. However, the earth is filled with rebellion. Satan takes the lead to rebel against God. But praise the Lord that in the midst of all this rebellion, there is a Body composed of those who have been redeemed and baptized into the Triune God! Baptism is not a formality. We have been baptized into the name of the Father, the Son, and the Holy Spirit (Matt. 28:19). According to Romans 6:3 and Galatians 3:27, we have been baptized into Christ. To be baptized into Christ as the life-giving Spirit brings us into the Body in an organic way. Thus, on earth there is an organism, the Body, constituted of those who have been redeemed and baptized into the Triune God. This is the Body of the One in heaven who submits Himself to God's headship. Now, on earth, this Body must reflect Christ's submission in the heavens.

The Body of Christ on earth should reflect Christ as the Head submitting Himself to the headship of God. We must be a heavenly television expressing on earth what is taking place in the heavens. Christ is the One who became a man, who was slain for our sins, and who was resurrected to become the life-giving Spirit so that we may have life. Now this One is in the heavens submitting Himself to God's headship for the carrying out of the divine administration....This means that the church in each locality must reflect the heavenly vision and express Christ's submission to the headship of God for the carrying out of His administration.

Does your local church reflect Christ's submission in the heavens? We praise the Lord that in many places there is a proper reflection of Christ's submission to the headship of God. Although the earth is filled with rebellion, we must be a people under God's headship reflecting through our submission to Christ His own submission to God. (*Life-study of 1 Corinthians,* pp. 477-478)

Further Reading: Life-study of 1 Corinthians, msg. 53; *The Collected Works of Watchman Nee,* vol. 50, ch. 44

Enlightenment and inspiration: _____

_____

_____

Morning Nourishment

1 Cor.   For He has subjected all things under His feet. But
15:27-28 when He says that all things are subjected, it is
         evident that *all things are* except Him who has
         subjected all things to Him. And when all things
         have been subjected to Him, then the Son Himself
         also will be subjected to Him who has subjected
         all things to Him, that God may be all in all.
Eph.   Unto the economy of the fullness of the times, to
1:10   head up all things in Christ, the things in the
         heavens and the things on the earth, in Him.

In 1 Corinthians 15:27 the phrase *His feet* and the second
Him refer to Christ as the Man prophesied in Psalm 8:4-8. To
Him—the resurrected, glorified, and exalted Man—God has
subjected all things (Heb. 2:7-9; Eph. 1:20-22). God has subjected all things under Christ's feet. However, it is evident that
this does not include God Himself. God, the One who has
subjected all things to Christ, is the only exception.

Verse 28...is the carrying out of God's administration by the
way of resurrection....Christ, as the Son of God to be the head
of man in His humanity, is under the headship of God the Father
(11:3). This is for God's governmental administration. After God
the Father has subjected all things under His feet as a resurrected
Man in glory (Eph. 1:22; Heb. 2:7-8), and after He as such a
resurrected Man has put all enemies under His feet to execute
God the Father's subjection of all things to Him, He as the Son
of God will also, along with His delivery of the kingdom back to
God the Father (1 Cor. 15:24), subject Himself in His divinity to God
the Father, who has subjected all things to Him the Son in His
humanity. This indicates the Son's absolute subjection and subordination to the Father, exalting the Father that God the Father
may be all in all. (*Life-study of 1 Corinthians,* pp. 602-603)

Today's Reading

At this point I would refer to Ephesians 1:10....How will God subject all things under Christ? He will do this by heading up all things in Christ. Furthermore, it is through the church that all things will be headed up in Christ. First, Christ must have the Body, the church. In His Body He must first head us up. We have seen that in 1 Corinthians 11:3 Paul says that the head of Christ is God, the head of every man is Christ, and the head of the woman is the man. The heading up first takes place in the church. The church is the Body for Christ the Head to head up all things. Once the church has been headed up, the church will be used by Christ as His Body to head up all things. This will be in resurrection.

In 11:3 Paul begins with the headship and in 15:24-28 he consummates with resurrection. In resurrection Christ not only became the life-giving Spirit to impart His life into His Body; He also became the reigning King to execute God's administration. All this is in resurrection. On the one hand, to us as God's chosen people, Christ in resurrection is the life-giving Spirit imparting life to us. On the other hand, to the nations, Christ in His resurrection has become the reigning King executing God's administration. His Body must cooperate with Him in His resurrection life and resurrection authority so that the church may be headed up. Then all the nations will be headed up. Moreover, as He is heading up all things, He is subduing, subjecting, His enemies under His feet. Eventually, at the end of the millennium, after the end of all the ages and dispensations, God's administration will be fully accomplished, and Christ will deliver the kingdom back to God, the One who subjected all things under Him. Then there will be the new heaven and the new earth, and we shall be in the New Jerusalem enjoying Christ and reigning with Him over the nations. This is God's administration carried out in Christ's all-inclusive resurrection. (*Life-study of 1 Corinthians*, pp. 603-604)

Further Reading: Life-study of 1 Corinthians, msg. 66

Enlightenment and inspiration: _____

_____

_____

_____

Hymns, #947

1 God's Kingdom today is a real exercise,
  But when Christ comes to reign it will be a great prize;
  It is wisdom divine that we now may be trained
  That His plan be fulfilled and His justice maintained.

2 God's children, we're born to be kings with His Son,
  And we need to be trained that we may overcome
  And to know how to rule in His kingdom as kings,
  That His kingship thru us be expressed o'er all things.

3 Today we must learn to submit to His throne,
  How to have a strict life and His government own;
  His authority then we'll be able to share,
  O'er the nations to rule with God's Son as the heir.

4 With a life strict to self we must righteousness hold,
  Kind to others in peace, and with God joyful, bold;
  In the Kingdom's reality e'er to remain,
  For its manifestation prepared thus to reign.

5 Then Christ when He comes with the kingdom from God
  Will to us grant His kingship to share as reward;
  Thus the Lord will His righteousness thru us maintain
  And His wisdom to heavenly powers make plain.

6 For this the Apostle pressed on at all cost,
  For the Kingdom assured that he would not be lost;
  'Tis for this he charged others, Be true to the Lord,
  That the Kingdom might be unto them a reward.

7 O Lord, give us grace for Thy Kingdom to live,
  To be trained that Thou may the reward to us give;
  Make the Kingdom's reality our exercise,
  That its manifestation may be our great prize.

Composition for prophecy with main point and sub-points: _____

_____

_____

_____

_____

_____

_____

_____

_____

_____

_____

_____

_____

_____

_____

_____

_____

_____

_____

_____

_____

_____

_____

_____

_____

_____

_____

_____

_____

_____

_____

_____

_____

_____

_____

_____

_____

_____

_____

_____

Reading Schedule for the Recovery Version of the New Testament with Footnotes

Wk.	Lord's Day	Monday	Tuesday	Wednesday	Thursday	Friday	Saturday
1	☐ Matt 1:1-2	☐ 1:3-7	☐ 1:8-17	☐ 1:18-25	☐ 2:1-23	☐ 3:1-6	☐ 3:7-17
2	☐ 4:1-11	☐ 4:12-25	☐ 5:1-4	☐ 5:5-12	☐ 5:13-20	☐ 5:21-26	☐ 5:27-48
3	☐ 6:1-8	☐ 6:9-18	☐ 6:19-34	☐ 7:1-12	☐ 7:13-29	☐ 8:1-13	☐ 8:14-22
4	☐ 8:23-34	☐ 9:1-13	☐ 9:14-17	☐ 9:18-34	☐ 9:35—10:5	☐ 10:6-25	☐ 10:26-42
5	☐ 11:1-15	☐ 11:16-30	☐ 12:1-14	☐ 12:15-32	☐ 12:33-42	☐ 12:43—13:2	☐ 13:3-12
6	☐ 13:13-30	☐ 13:31-43	☐ 13:44-58	☐ 14:1-13	☐ 14:14-21	☐ 14:22-36	☐ 15:1-20
7	☐ 15:21-31	☐ 15:32-39	☐ 16:1-12	☐ 16:13-20	☐ 16:21-28	☐ 17:1-13	☐ 17:14-27
8	☐ 18:1-14	☐ 18:15-22	☐ 18:23-35	☐ 19:1-15	☐ 19:16-30	☐ 20:1-16	☐ 20:17-34
9	☐ 21:1-11	☐ 21:12-22	☐ 21:23-32	☐ 21:33-46	☐ 22:1-22	☐ 22:23-33	☐ 22:34-46
10	☐ 23:1-12	☐ 23:13-39	☐ 24:1-14	☐ 24:15-31	☐ 24:32-51	☐ 25:1-13	☐ 25:14-30
11	☐ 25:31-46	☐ 26:1-16	☐ 26:17-35	☐ 26:36-46	☐ 26:47-64	☐ 26:65-75	☐ 27:1-26
12	☐ 27:27-44	☐ 27:45-56	☐ 27:57—28:15	☐ 28:16-20	☐ Mark 1:1	☐ 1:2-6	☐ 1:7-13
13	☐ 1:14-28	☐ 1:29-45	☐ 2:1-12	☐ 2:13-28	☐ 3:1-19	☐ 3:20-35	☐ 4:1-25
14	☐ 4:26-41	☐ 5:1-20	☐ 5:21-43	☐ 6:1-29	☐ 6:30-56	☐ 7:1-23	☐ 7:24-37
15	☐ 8:1-26	☐ 8:27—9:1	☐ 9:2-29	☐ 9:30-50	☐ 10:1-16	☐ 10:17-34	☐ 10:35-52
16	☐ 11:1-16	☐ 11:17-33	☐ 12:1-27	☐ 12:28-44	☐ 13:1-13	☐ 13:14-37	☐ 14:1-26
17	☐ 14:27-52	☐ 14:53-72	☐ 15:1-15	☐ 15:16-47	☐ 16:1-8	☐ 16:9-20	☐ Luke 1:1-4
18	☐ 1:5-25	☐ 1:26-46	☐ 1:47-56	☐ 1:57-80	☐ 2:1-8	☐ 2:9-20	☐ 2:21-39
19	☐ 2:40-52	☐ 3:1-20	☐ 3:21-38	☐ 4:1-13	☐ 4:14-30	☐ 4:31-44	☐ 5:1-26
20	☐ 5:27—6:16	☐ 6:17-38	☐ 6:39-49	☐ 7:1-17	☐ 7:18-23	☐ 7:24-35	☐ 7:36-50
21	☐ 8:1-15	☐ 8:16-25	☐ 8:26-39	☐ 8:40-56	☐ 9:1-17	☐ 9:18-26	☐ 9:27-36
22	☐ 9:37-50	☐ 9:51-62	☐ 10:1-11	☐ 10:12-24	☐ 10:25-37	☐ 10:38-42	☐ 11:1-13
23	☐ 11:14-26	☐ 11:27-36	☐ 11:37-54	☐ 12:1-12	☐ 12:13-21	☐ 12:22-34	☐ 12:35-48
24	☐ 12:49-59	☐ 13:1-9	☐ 13:10-17	☐ 13:18-30	☐ 13:31—14:6	☐ 14:7-14	☐ 14:15-24
25	☐ 14:25-35	☐ 15:1-10	☐ 15:11-21	☐ 15:22-32	☐ 16:1-13	☐ 16:14-22	☐ 16:23-31
26	☐ 17:1-19	☐ 17:20-37	☐ 18:1-14	☐ 18:15-30	☐ 18:31-43	☐ 19:1-10	☐ 19:11-27

Reading Schedule for the Recovery Version of the New Testament with Footnotes

Wk.	Lord's Day	Monday	Tuesday	Wednesday	Thursday	Friday	Saturday
27	Luke 19:28-48	20:1-19	20:20-38	20:39—21:4	21:5-27	21:28-38	22:1-20
28	22:21-38	22:39-54	22:55-71	23:1-43	23:44-56	24:1-12	24:13-35
29	24:36-53	John 1:1-13	1:14-18	1:19-34	1:35-51	2:1-11	2:12-22
30	2:23—3:13	3:14-21	3:22-36	4:1-14	4:15-26	4:27-42	4:43-54
31	5:1-16	5:17-30	5:31-47	6:1-15	6:16-31	6:32-51	6:52-71
32	7:1-9	7:10-24	7:25-36	7:37-52	7:53—8:11	8:12-27	8:28-44
33	8:45-59	9:1-13	9:14-34	9:35—10:9	10:10-30	10:31—11:4	11:5-22
34	11:23-40	11:41-57	12:1-11	12:12-24	12:25-36	12:37-50	13:1-11
35	13:12-30	13:31-38	14:1-6	14:7-20	14:21-31	15:1-11	15:12-27
36	16:1-15	16:16-33	17:1-5	17:6-13	17:14-24	17:25—18:11	18:12-27
37	18:28-40	19:1-16	19:17-30	19:31-42	20:1-13	20:14-18	20:19-22
38	20:23-31	21:1-14	21:15-22	21:23-25	Acts 1:1-8	1:9-14	1:15-26
39	2:1-13	2:14-21	2:22-36	2:37-41	2:42-47	3:1-18	3:19—4:22
40	4:23-37	5:1-16	5:17-32	5:33-42	6:1—7:1	7:2-29	7:30-60
41	8:1-13	8:14-25	8:26-40	9:1-19	9:20-43	10:1-16	10:17-33
42	10:34-48	11:1-18	11:19-30	12:1-25	13:1-12	13:13-43	13:44—14:5
43	14:6-28	15:1-12	15:13-34	15:35—16:5	16:6-18	16:19-40	17:1-18
44	17:19-34	18:1-17	18:18-28	19:1-20	19:21-41	20:1-12	20:13-38
45	21:1-14	21:15-26	21:27-40	22:1-21	22:22-29	22:30—23:11	23:12-15
46	23:16-30	23:31—24:21	24:22—25:5	25:6-27	26:1-13	26:14-32	27:1-26
47	27:27—28:10	28:11-22	28:23-31	Rom 1:1-2	1:3-7	1:8-17	1:18-25
48	1:26—2:10	2:11-29	3:1-20	3:21-31	4:1-12	4:13-25	5:1-11
49	5:12-17	5:18—6:5	6:6-11	6:12-23	7:1-12	7:13-25	8:1-2
50	8:3-6	8:7-13	8:14-25	8:26-39	9:1-18	9:19—10:3	10:4-15
51	10:16—11:10	11:11-22	11:23-36	12:1-3	12:4-21	13:1-14	14:1-12
52	14:13-23	15:1-13	15:14-33	16:1-5	16:6-24	16:25-27	I Cor 1:1-4

Reading Schedule for the Recovery Version of the New Testament with Footnotes

Wk.	Lord's Day	Monday	Tuesday	Wednesday	Thursday	Friday	Saturday
53	I Cor 1:5-9	1:10-17	1:18-31	2:1-5	2:6-10	2:11-16	3:1-9
54	3:10-13	3:14-23	4:1-9	4:10-21	5:1-13	6:1-11	6:12-20
55	7:1-16	7:17-24	7:25-40	8:1-13	9:1-15	9:16-27	10:1-4
56	10:5-13	10:14-33	11:1-6	11:7-16	11:17-26	11:27-34	12:1-11
57	12:12-22	12:23-31	13:1-13	14:1-12	14:13-25	14:26-33	14:34-40
58	15:1-19	15:20-28	15:29-34	15:35-49	15:50-58	16:1-9	16:10-24
59	II Cor 1:1-4	1:5-14	1:15-22	1:23—2:11	2:12-17	3:1-6	3:7-11
60	3:12-18	4:1-6	4:7-12	4:13-18	5:1-8	5:9-15	5:16-21
61	6:1-13	6:14—7:4	7:5-16	8:1-15	8:16-24	9:1-15	10:1-6
62	10:7-18	11:1-15	11:16-33	12:1-10	12:11-21	13:1-10	13:11-14
63	Gal 1:1-5	1:6-14	1:15-24	2:1-13	2:14-21	3:1-4	3:5-14
64	3:15-22	3:23-29	4:1-7	4:8-20	4:21-31	5:1-12	5:13-21
65	5:22-26	6:1-10	6:11-15	6:16-18	Eph 1:1-3	1:4-6	1:7-10
66	1:11-14	1:15-18	1:19-23	2:1-5	2:6-10	2:11-14	2:15-18
67	2:19-22	3:1-7	3:8-13	3:14-18	3:19-21	4:1-4	4:5-10
68	4:11-16	4:17-24	4:25-32	5:1-10	5:11-21	5:22-26	5:27-33
69	6:1-9	6:10-14	6:15-18	6:19-24	Phil 1:1-7	1:8-18	1:19-26
70	1:27—2:4	2:5-11	2:12-16	2:17-30	3:1-6`	3:7-11	3:12-16
71	3:17-21	4:1-9	4:10-23	Col 1:1-8	1:9-13	1:14-23	1:24-29
72	2:1-7	2:8-15	2:16-23	3:1-4	3:5-15	3:16-25	4:1-18
73	I Thes 1:1-3	1:4-10	2:1-12	2:13—3:5	3:6-13	4:1-10	4:11—5:11
74	5:12-28	II Thes 1:1-12	2:1-17	3:1-18	I Tim 1:1-2	1:3-4	1:5-14
75	1:15-20	2:1-7	2:8-15	3:1-13	3:14—4:5	4:6-16	5:1-25
76	6:1-10	6:11-21	II Tim 1:1-10	1:11-18	2:1-15	2:16-26	3:1-13
77	3:14—4:8	4:9-22	Titus 1:1-4	1:5-16	2:1-15	3:1-8	3:9-15
78	Philem 1:1-11	1:12-25	Heb 1:1-2	1:3-5	1:6-14	2:1-9	2:10-18

Reading Schedule for the Recovery Version of the New Testament with Footnotes

Wk.	Lord's Day	Monday	Tuesday	Wednesday	Thursday	Friday	Saturday
79	Heb 3:1-6	3:7-19	4:1-9	4:10-13	4:14-16	5:1-10	5:11—6:3
80	6:4-8	6:9-20	7:1-10	7:11-28	8:1-6	8:7-13	9:1-4
81	9:5-14	9:15-28	10:1-18	10:19-28	10:29-39	11:1-6	11:7-19
82	11:20-31	11:32-40	12:1-2	12:3-13	12:14-17	12:18-26	12:27-29
83	13:1-7	13:8-12	13:13-15	13:16-25	James1:1-8	1:9-18	1:19-27
84	2:1-13	2:14-26	3:1-18	4:1-10	4:11-17	5:1-12	5:13-20
85	I Pet 1:1-2	1:3-4	1:5	1:6-9	1:10-12	1:13-17	1:18-25
86	2:1-3	2:4-8	2:9-17	2:18-25	3:1-13	3:14-22	4:1-6
87	4:7-16	4:17-19	5:1-4	5:5-9	5:10-14	II Pet 1:1-2	1:3-4
88	1:5-8	1:9-11	1:12-18	1:19-21	2:1-3	2:4-11	2:12-22
89	3:1-6	3:7-9	3:10-12	3:13-15	3:16	3:17-18	I John 1:1-2
90	1:3-4	1:5	1:6	1:7	1:8-10	2:1-2	2:3-11
91	2:12-14	2:15-19	2:20-23	2:24-27	2:28-29	3:1-5	3:6-10
92	3:11-18	3:19-24	4:1-6	4:7-11	4:12-15	4:16—5:3	5:4-13
93	5:14-17	5:18-21	II John 1:1-3	1:4-9	1:10-13	III John 1:1-6	1:7-14
94	Jude 1:1-4	1:5-10	1:11-19	1:20-25	Rev 1:1-3	1:4-6	1:7-11
95	1:12-13	1:14-16	1:17-20	2:1-6	2:7	2:8-9	2:10-11
96	2:12-14	2:15-17	2:18-23	2:24-29	3:1-3	3:4-6	3:7-9
97	3:10-13	3:14-18	3:19-22	4:1-5	4:6-7	4:8-11	5:1-6
98	5:7-14	6:1-8	6:9-17	7:1-8	7:9-17	8:1-6	8:7-12
99	8:13—9:11	9:12-21	10:1-4	10:5-11	11:1-4	11:5-14	11:15-19
100	12:1-4	12:5-9	12:10-18	13:1-10	13:11-18	14:1-5	14:6-12
101	14:13-20	15:1-8	16:1-12	16:13-21	17:1-6	17:7-18	18:1-8
102	18:9—19:4	19:5-10	19:11-16	19:17-21	20:1-6	20:7-10	20:11-15
103	21:1	21:2	21:3-8	21:9-13	21:14-18	21:19-21	21:22-27
104	22:1	22:2	22:3-11	22:12-15	22:16-17	22:18-21	

Week 1 — Day 1

1 Cor. 2:2 For I did not determine to know anything among you except Jesus Christ, and this One crucified.

1 Cor. 1:2 To the church of God which is in Corinth, to those who have been sanctified in Christ Jesus, the called saints, with all those who call upon the name of our Lord Jesus Christ in every place, *who is* theirs and ours.

Col. 1:12 Giving thanks to the Father, who has qualified you for a share of the allotted portion of the saints in the light.

_____
Date

Week 1 — Day 2

1 Cor. 1:9 God is faithful, through whom you were called into the fellowship of His Son, Jesus Christ our Lord.

6:17 But he who is joined to the Lord is one spirit.

_____
Date

Week 1 — Day 3

1 Cor. 1:9 God is faithful, through whom you were called into the fellowship of His Son, Jesus Christ our Lord.

Phil. 2:18 And in like manner you also rejoice, and you rejoice together with me.

4:4 Rejoice in the Lord always; again I will say, rejoice.

_____
Date

Week 1 — Day 4

Acts 2:42 And they continued steadfastly in the teaching and the fellowship of the apostles, in the breaking of bread and the prayers.

1 John 1:3 That which we have seen and heard we report also to you that you also may have fellowship with us, and indeed our fellowship is with the Father and with His Son Jesus Christ.

2 Cor. 13:14 The grace of the Lord Jesus Christ and the love of God and the fellowship of the Holy Spirit be with you all.

_____
Date

Week 1 — Day 5

1 Cor. 1:2 To the church of God which is in Corinth, to those who have been sanctified in Christ Jesus, the called saints, with all those who call upon the name of our Lord Jesus Christ in every place, *who is* theirs and ours.

9-10 God is faithful, through whom you were called into the fellowship of His Son, Jesus Christ our Lord. Now I beseech you, brothers, through the name of our Lord Jesus Christ, that you all speak the same thing and *that* there be no divisions among you, but *that* you be attuned in the same mind and in the same opinion.

12 ...Each of you says, I am of Paul, and I of Apollos, and I of Cephas, and I of Christ.

_____
Date

Week 1 — Day 6

1 Cor. 1:10 Now I beseech you, brothers, through the name of our Lord Jesus Christ, that you all speak the same thing and *that* there be no divisions among you, but *that* you be attuned in the same mind and in the same opinion.

Col. 3:11 Where there cannot be Greek and Jew, circumcision and uncircumcision, barbarian, Scythian, slave, free man, but Christ is all and in all.

Phil. 2:2 Make my joy full, that you think the same thing, having the same love, joined in soul, thinking the one thing.

Rom. 15:6 That with one accord you may with one mouth glorify the God and Father of our Lord Jesus Christ.

_____
Date

Week 2 — Day 6 — Today's verses

1 Cor. 2:9-10 But as it is written, "Things which eye has not seen and ear has not heard and *which* have not come up in man's heart; things which God has prepared for those who love Him." But to us God has revealed *them* through the Spirit, for the Spirit searches all things, even the depths of God.

Psa. 73:25 Whom do I have in heaven *but You?* And besides You there is nothing I desire on earth.

25:14 The intimate counsel of Jehovah is to those who fear Him, and His covenant will He make known to them.

_____
Date

Week 2 — Day 3 — Today's verses

1 Cor. 1:18 For the word of the cross is to those who are perishing foolishness, but to us who are being saved it is the power of God.

24 But to those who are called, both Jews and Greeks, Christ the power of God and the wisdom of God.

Phil. 4:8 Finally, brothers, what things are true, what things are dignified, what things are righteous, what things are pure, what things are lovely, what things are well spoken of, if there is any virtue and if any praise, take account of these things.

13 I am able to do all things in Him who empowers me.

_____
Date

Week 2 — Day 5 — Today's verses

Exo. 15:23 And when they came to Marah, they could not drink of the waters of Marah, for they were bitter; therefore its name was called Marah.

25-26 And he cried out to Jehovah, and Jehovah showed him a tree; and he cast it into the waters, and the waters became sweet. There He made for them a statute and an ordinance, and there He tested them. And He said,...I am Jehovah who heals you.

1 Pet. 2:24 Who Himself bore up our sins in His body on the tree, in order that we, having died to sins, might live to righteousness; by whose bruise you were healed.

_____
Date

Week 2 — Day 2 — Today's verses

1 Cor. 5:7-8 Purge out the old leaven that you may be a new lump, even as you are unleavened; for our Passover, Christ, also has been sacrificed. So then let us keep the feast, not with old leaven, neither with the leaven of malice and evil, but with the unleavened *bread* of sincerity and truth.

10:3-4 And all ate the same spiritual food, and all drank the same spiritual drink; for they drank of a spiritual rock which followed *them*, and the rock was Christ.

_____
Date

Week 2 — Day 4 — Today's verses

1 Cor. 1:30 But of Him you are in Christ Jesus, who became wisdom to us from God: both righteousness and sanctification and redemption.

Rom. 8:10 But if Christ is in you,...the spirit is life because of righteousness.

6:22 But now, having been freed from sin and enslaved to God, you have your fruit unto sanctification, and the end, eternal life.

8:23 ...We...who have the firstfruits of the Spirit, even we ourselves groan in ourselves, eagerly awaiting sonship, the redemption of our body.

_____
Date

Week 2 — Day 1 — Today's verses

1 Cor. 2:2 For I did not determine to know anything among you except Jesus Christ, and this One crucified.

1:23 But we preach Christ crucified, to Jews a stumbling block, and to Gentiles foolishness.

Gal. 2:20 I am crucified with Christ; and *it is* no longer I *who* live, but *it is* Christ *who* lives in me; and the *life* which I now live in the flesh I live in faith, the *faith* of the Son of God, who loved me and gave Himself up for me.

_____
Date

Week 3 — Day 4   Today's verses

Rom. For God is my witness, whom I serve in
1:9 my spirit in the gospel of His Son....

8:16 The Spirit Himself witnesses with our spirit that we are children of God.

1 Cor. But he who is joined to the Lord is one
6:17 spirit.

2 Cor. I had no rest in my spirit, for I did not find
2:13 Titus my brother...

13:14 The grace of the Lord Jesus Christ and the love of God and the fellowship of the Holy Spirit be with you all.

_____
Date

Week 3 — Day 5   Today's verses

1 Cor. But to us God has revealed *them* through
2:10-11 the Spirit, for the Spirit searches all things, even the depths of God. For who among men knows the things of man, except the spirit of man which is in him? In the same way, the things of God also no one has known except the Spirit of God.

Mark And immediately Jesus, knowing fully in
2:8 His spirit that they were reasoning this way within themselves...

_____
Date

Week 3 — Day 6   Today's verses

1 Cor. A man should account us in this way, as
4:1 servants of Christ and stewards of the mysteries of God.

2:13 Which things also we speak, not in words taught by human wisdom but in words taught by the Spirit, interpreting spiritual things with spiritual *words*.

16 For who has known the mind of the Lord and will instruct Him? But we have the mind of Christ.

_____
Date

Week 3 — Day 1   Today's verses

1 Cor. But a soulish man does not receive the
2:14-15 things of the Spirit of God, for they are foolishness to him and he is not able to know *them* because they are discerned spiritually. But the spiritual man discerns all things, but he himself is discerned by no one.

3:1 And I, brothers, was not able to speak to you as to spiritual men, but as to fleshy, as to infants in Christ.

6:17 But he who is joined to the Lord is one spirit.

Gal. If we live by the Spirit, let us also walk by
5:25 the Spirit.

_____
Date

Week 3 — Day 2   Today's verses

1 Cor. Do you not know that you are the temple
3:16 of God, and *that* the Spirit of God dwells in you?

2 Tim. The Lord be with your spirit. Grace be
4:22 with you.

Heb. Having therefore, brothers, boldness for
10:19 entering the *Holy* of Holies in the blood of Jesus.

_____
Date

Week 3 — Day 3   Today's verses

Gen. On that day Jehovah made a covenant
15:18 with Abram, saying, To your seed do I give this land...

Deut. And you shall do that which is right and
6:18 good in the sight of Jehovah so that it may go well with you and you may enter and possess the good land, concerning which Jehovah swore to your fathers.

Gal. In order that the blessing of Abraham
3:14 might come to the Gentiles in Christ Jesus, that we might receive the promise of the Spirit through faith.

2 Tim. The Lord be with your spirit. Grace be
4:22 with you.

_____
Date

Week 4 — Day 1

Today's verses

1 Cor. 3:2 I gave you milk to drink, not solid food, for you were not yet able to receive it. But neither yet now are you able.

1 Cor. 3:6 I planted, Apollos watered, but God caused the growth.

Col. 2:19 And not holding the Head, out from whom all the Body, being richly supplied and knit together by means of the joints and sinews, grows with the growth of God.

_____
Date

Week 4 — Day 2

Today's verses

1 Cor. 1:7 So that you do not lack in any gift, eagerly awaiting the revelation of our Lord Jesus Christ.

1 Cor. 3:7 So then neither is he who plants anything nor he who waters, but God who causes the growth.

Rom. 6:23 For the wages of sin is death, but the gift of God is eternal life in Christ Jesus our Lord.

Acts 2:38 And Peter said to them, Repent and each one of you be baptized upon the name of Jesus Christ for the forgiveness of your sins, and you will receive the gift of the Holy Spirit.

_____
Date

Week 4 — Day 3

Today's verses

1 Cor. 3:6 I planted, Apollos watered, but God caused the growth.

1 Cor. 3:9 For we are God's fellow workers; you are God's cultivated land, God's building.

Eph. 4:15 But holding to truth in love, we may grow up into Him in all things, who is the Head, Christ.

Gal. 4:19 My children, with whom I travail again in birth until Christ is formed in you.

_____
Date

Week 4 — Day 4

Today's verses

1 Cor. 3:9 ...You are God's cultivated land, God's building.

1 Cor. 3:12 But if anyone builds upon the foundation gold, silver, precious stones, wood, grass, stubble.

2 Pet. 1:4 ...That through these you might become partakers of the divine nature...

2 Cor. 3:18 But we all with unveiled face, beholding and reflecting like a mirror the glory of the Lord, are being transformed into the same image from glory to glory, even as from the Lord Spirit.

_____
Date

Week 4 — Day 5

Today's verses

1 Cor. 3:12 But if anyone builds upon the foundation gold, silver, precious stones, wood, grass, stubble.

1 Cor. 3:16 Do you not know that you are the temple of God, and that the Spirit of God dwells in you?

Eph. 3:17 That Christ may make His home in your hearts through faith, that you, being rooted and grounded in love.

_____
Date

Week 4 — Day 6

Today's verses

1 Cor. 3:16 Do you not know that you are the temple of God, and that the Spirit of God dwells in you?

1 Cor. 3:9 ...You are God's cultivated land, God's building.

Eph. 2:21 In whom all the building, being fitted together, is growing into a holy temple in the Lord.

Eph. 4:16 Out from whom all the Body, being joined together and being knit together through every joint of the rich supply and through the operation in the measure of each one part, causes the growth of the Body unto the building up of itself in love.

_____
Date

Week 5 — Day 6 · Today's verses

1 Cor. 7:10 But to the married I charge, not I but the Lord, A wife must not be separated from her husband.

25 Now concerning virgins I have no commandment of the Lord, but I give my opinion as one who has been shown mercy by the Lord to be faithful.

40 But she is more blessed if she so remains, according to my opinion; but I think that I also have the Spirit of God.

Gal. 2:20 I am crucified with Christ; and it is no longer I who live, but it is Christ who lives in me...

_____
Date

Week 5 — Day 3 · Today's verses

1 Cor. 6:17 But he who is joined to the Lord is one spirit.

Rom. 8:16 The Spirit Himself witnesses with our spirit that we are children of God.

John 1:13 Who were begotten not of blood, nor of the will of the flesh, nor of the will of man, but of God.

3:6 That which is born of the flesh is flesh, and that which is born of the Spirit is spirit.

Phil. 1:21 For to me, to live is Christ...

_____
Date

Week 5 — Day 5 · Today's verses

John 15:4-5 Abide in Me and I in you. As the branch cannot bear fruit of itself unless it abides in the vine, so neither can you unless you abide in Me. I am the vine; you are the branches. He who abides in Me and I in him, he bears much fruit; for apart from Me you can do nothing.

1 Cor. 7:12 But to the rest I say, I, not the Lord, If any brother has an unbelieving wife and she consents to dwell with him, he must not leave her.

_____
Date

Week 5 — Day 2 · Today's verses

1 Cor. 6:14-15 And God has both raised up the Lord and will raise us up through His power. Do you not know that your bodies are members of Christ?...

17 But he who is joined to the Lord is one spirit.

19-20 Or do you not know that your body is a temple of the Holy Spirit within you, whom you have from God, and you are not your own? For you have been bought with a price. So then glorify God in your body.

_____
Date

Week 5 — Day 4 · Today's verses

1 Cor. 7:17 However as the Lord has apportioned to each one, as God has called each one, so let him walk. And so I direct in all the churches.

20-21 Each one, in the calling in which he was called, in this let him remain. Were you called as a slave? Let it not concern you; but even if you are able to become free, use your status as a slave rather.

24 Each one, brothers, in what status he was called, in this let him remain with God.

_____
Date

Week 5 — Day 1 · Today's verses

1 Cor. 6:17 But he who is joined to the Lord is one spirit.

19 ...Your body is a temple of the Holy Spirit within you...

John 3:6 ...That which is born of the Spirit is spirit.

That every one who believes into Him may have eternal life.

Rom. 8:4 That the righteous requirement of the law might be fulfilled in us, who...walk...according to the spirit.

6 ...The mind set on the spirit is life and peace.

_____
Date

Week 6 — Day 1

Today's verses

1 Cor. 9:23-25
And I do all things for the sake of the gospel that I may become a fellow partaker of it. Do you not know that those who run in a racecourse all run, but one receives the prize? Run in this way, that you may lay hold. And everyone who contends exercises self-control in all things; they then, that they may receive a corruptible crown, but we, an incorruptible.

2 Tim. 4:7-8
I have fought the good fight; I have finished the course; I have kept the faith. Henceforth there is laid up for me the crown of righteousness, with which the Lord, the righteous Judge, will recompense me in that day, and not only me but also all those who have loved His appearing.

Date

Week 6 — Day 2

Today's verses

1 Cor. 9:26-27
I therefore run in this way, not as though without a clear aim; I box in this way, not as though beating the air; but I buffet my body and make it my slave, lest perhaps having preached to others, I myself may become disapproved.

Matt. 7:21-23
Not every one who says to Me, Lord, Lord, will enter into the kingdom of the heavens, but he who does the will of My Father who is in the heavens. Many will say to Me in that day; Lord, Lord, *was it* not in Your name *that* we prophesied, and in Your name cast out demons, and in Your name did many works of power? And then I will declare to them: I never knew you. Depart from Me, you workers of lawlessness.

Date

Week 6 — Day 3

Today's verses

1 Cor. 10:5-6
But with most of them God was not well pleased, for they were strewn along in the wilderness. Now these things occurred as examples to us, that we should not be ones who lust after evil things, even as they lusted.

11
Now these things happened to them as an example, and they were written for our admonition, unto whom the ends of the ages have come.

Phil. 3:13-14
Brothers, I do not account of myself to have laid hold; but one thing *I do:* Forgetting the things which are behind and stretching forward to the things which are before, I pursue toward the goal for the prize to which God in Christ Jesus has called *me* upward.

Date

Week 6 — Day 4

Today's verses

1 Cor. 3:11-12
For another foundation no one is able to lay besides that which is laid, which is Jesus Christ. But if anyone builds upon the foundation gold, silver, precious stones, wood, grass, stubble.

14-15
If anyone's work which he has built upon *the foundation* remains, he will receive a reward; if anyone's work is consumed, he will suffer loss, but he himself will be saved, yet so as through fire.

17
If anyone destroys the temple of God, God will destroy him; for the temple of God is holy, *and* such are you.

Date

Week 6 — Day 5

Today's verses

1 Cor. 11:3
But I want you to know that Christ is the head of every man, and the man is the head of the woman, and God is the head of Christ.

Eph. 1:10
Unto the economy of the fullness of the times, to head up all things in Christ, the things in the heavens and the things on the earth, in Him.

5:23
For a husband is head of the wife as also Christ is Head of the church, He Himself *being* the Savior of the Body.

Date

Week 6 — Day 6

Today's verses

1 Cor. 15:27-28
For He has subjected all things under His feet. But when He says that all things are subjected, it is evident that *all things are* except Him who has subjected all things to Him. And when all things have been subjected to Him, then the Son Himself also will be subjected to Him who has subjected all things to Him, that God may be all in all.

Eph. 1:10
Unto the economy of the fullness of the times, to head up all things in Christ, the things in the heavens and the things on the earth, in Him.

Date